The Promise
of
H. Richard Niebuhr

The Promise
of
H. Richard Niebuhr

by
JOHN D. GODSEY

J. B. LIPPINCOTT COMPANY
Philadelphia and New York

In Memoriam

William Clinton Godsey
William Clinton Godsey, Jr.
Edwin Shirley Godsey

Foreword

Helmut Richard Niebuhr was an economical thinker. In person he took no pains to splatter elements of charisma on classroom or audience. In his writing there is no dazzle of anecdotes, no moment of meandering, no waste of the linotypist's or the reader's time. His writings are clear, brief, honed, and sometimes almost austere. He was a refined lecturer more than a prophetic preacher.

The legacy of Niebuhr, however, is among the richest in American theology in the twentieth century; as a matter of fact, I wonder whether since Jonathan Edwards there has been a systematic theologian of such organizing brilliance as H. Richard Niebuhr. As a historian, I often look back on his long essay in *The Church Against the World* as being the most potent critique of an accommodated and acculturated faith in the 1930's. A person may criticize details of *Christ and Culture*, but he is not likely to be able to think his way around its categories, once they are stamped on his mind. Who in American theology has raised more issues in less space than he did in *The Meaning of Revelation?* I still assign my classes his *The Kingdom of God in America* as the book whose interpretation of our past is most worth arguing with and about.

Niebuhr's inheritance is durable. Not one of his books is really dated or obsolete, even though he tried to qualify people's enthusiasm for his first book and, in effect, wrote the best critique of it yet to appear. Responsive to the worlds of Karl Barth and Ernst Troeltsch, he fused the troubling questions of revelation and relativism, monotheism in faith and pluralism in culture into a combination that at times blends, at others creates tension, and in every case inspires others to do their own thinking.

Part of the promise of Niebuhr lies in his enduring ability to draw other people into personal formulation. One evidence of that ability is the cluster of students he nurtured at Yale Divinity School. Other theological giants of the century were notoriously poor teachers; still others had slavish disciples and followers. H. R. Niebuhr developed a group of men who are now at mid-career, people who differ from each other considerably, thinkers who have not lost their own individuality or given us mere carbon copies of his work. They are united only in the fact that their constructive thought and writing is based on their common experience of studying under him. As Professor Godsey makes clear, the writings of Niebuhr can still serve as teachers, and another generation can profit from his treatment of themes that are as urgent now as when he took them up.

MARTIN E. MARTY
The University of Chicago

Contents

I

The Man and His Work

When the curtain is rung down on the twentieth-century drama of church history in America and the critics have written their reviews, the family name of Niebuhr will surely stand out prominently among the stars. One might say that what the Barrymores have been to the theater, the Niebuhrs have been to the theological community. The spotlight focuses first on Hulda, the eldest and the only daughter in a family of five children, who for many years was Professor of Christian Education at McCormick Theological Seminary in Chicago. Attention next shifts to Reinhold, who from 1928 until his retirement in 1960 led the theological revival in America from his prestigious post as Professor of Applied Christianity at Union Theological Seminary in New York City. Then comes H. Richard, two years his brother's junior and the youngest in the family, who held an equally prestigious chair in Christian Ethics at Yale University's Divinity School from 1931 until his death in 1962. Finally, the family tradition is being carried on by the latter's son, Richard Reinhold, who presently serves Harvard Divinity School as Professor of Systematic Theology.

What lies behind this remarkable familial contribution to the church and to the culture at large? Surely it would be no exaggeration to say that in the Niebuhr family there emerged a creative blending of Germany's stringent academic tradition and America's penchant for social relevance. The parents, Gustav and Lydia Niebuhr, were both

German-Americans. Gustav immigrated from northwestern Germany at the age of seventeen and settled in the midwestern section of the United States, together with many of his countrymen who sought liberality in America after the German revolution of 1848. Through the support of an interested farmer he was enabled to study at Eden Theological Seminary and to enter the ministry of the German Evangelical Synod of North America, a church that stemmed from the Old Prussian Union in the old country. In his first parish, a mission outpost in San Francisco, Gustav married Lydia Hosto, the daughter of a fellow minister who also had a German background, and to this couple were born a daughter and four sons, one of whom died in infancy.

Helmut Richard Niebuhr was born at Wright City, Missouri, on September 3, 1894. He was reared in the bosom of a happy family which cherished the rich cultural heritage from Germany and yet entered zestfully and wholeheartedly into the new life of a swiftly developing country. The unaffected piety of his home, the inculcated sense of responsibility, the native intelligence, the winsome personality—all of these seemed to favor his decision as a young man to follow his father and his brother Reinhold into the ministry of the church. In preparation for this vocation he attended Elmhurst College in Illinois, a small school that was supported by his denomination but which at that time had not yet received accreditation. After receiving the Bachelor of Arts degree in 1912, he enrolled at Eden Theological Seminary, located near St. Louis, where he remained until graduation in 1915. The following year he was ordained a minister of the Evangelical Synod and became pastor of a congregation in St. Louis, which he served for the next two years. During this time he undertook new studies at Washington University and was granted a Master of Arts degree from this institution in 1917.

Niebuhr returned to Eden Seminary as a teacher in 1919, soon became engaged, and in June of the following year was married to Florence Marie Mittendorff, who became his companion through life and who later bore their two children, Cynthia and Richard Reinhold. In 1922 he left Eden in order to further his education at Yale University, from which he received a Bachelor of Divinity degree in 1923 and a Doctor of Philosophy in 1924. After graduation he became president of Elmhurst College and during a three-year tenure helped the school to become fully accredited. Although he possessed considerable administrative skill, Niebuhr felt himself drawn to the task of theological education, so in 1927 he returned to Eden, where he taught until he accepted the position of Associate Professor of Christian Ethics at Yale Divinity School in 1931. During his long and distinguished career at Yale, Niebuhr was elevated to a full professorship in 1938, was named Director of Graduate Studies in Religion in the Graduate School in 1953, and was honored in 1954 with the coveted title of Sterling Professor of Theology and Christian Ethics.

Throughout his career Niebuhr remained a dedicated churchman. He was an early advocate of church union and witnessed in 1934 the uniting of his own Evangelical Synod with a Reformed group to form the Evangelical and Reformed Church and then in 1957 saw this church unite with the Congregational Christian Churches of America to form a new body known as the United Church of Christ. His first book, *The Social Sources of Denominationalism*, declared denominationalism to be a fateful compromise of the church with the world, and it is not surprising that Niebuhr contributed not only a number of pertinent articles concerning the structure, norm, and mission of the church, but also major essays in preparation for both the first and the second assemblies of the World Council of Churches.

Congruent with his churchmanship was Niebuhr's dedication to the task of educating young men and women for the Christian ministry. Although not as ebullient and powerful a lecturer as his brother Reinhold, H. Richard gained the reputation of being a more careful and penetrating scholar. With keen insight, wry humor, and numerous facial contortions, he would develop and agonizingly appraise divergent viewpoints on a theological or ethical issue, with the result that his students were caught up in the workings of a great mind and through this experience learned how to think for themselves. Over the years his influence extended to a myriad of students who sat at his feet and then went on to become effective pastors and teachers throughout the world. Through his writings he influenced hosts of others and helped to educate a whole generation of Americans in the meaning of faith and in the understanding of their responsibilities under God.

Because of his eminence as a teacher and his intimate and long association with theological education Niebuhr was asked by the American Association of Theological Schools to direct a study of theological education in the United States and Canada during the years 1954-1955. With the aid of two associates, Daniel Day Williams and James M. Gustafson, and a staff of workers, he carried out an intensive inquiry into the trends and status of theological education in the majority of Protestant schools in the two nations. The results of this study, which was financed by the Carnegie Corporation of New York, were published in several bulletins and in two books: Niebuhr's *The Purpose of the Church and Its Ministry*, which dealt with the aims of theological education, and a companion volume entitled *The Advancement of Theological Education*, a summary report dealing with the methods of theological education and authored jointly by Niebuhr, Williams, and Gustafson. Another related book, *The Ministry in Historical Perspective*, was edited by Niebuhr and Williams. The entire project benefited immeasurably from Niebuhr's characteristic blending of exacting research and prophetic insight, and every theological school has felt the challenge of his definition of the goal of the church as "the increase among men of the love of God and neighbor" and of his conception of the ordained minister as "the pastoral director."

The essence of Niebuhr's thought as a practicing churchman and educator has been bequeathed to posterity in his writings. His legacy as an author includes eight books, including his dissertation at Yale; three brochures containing special lectures; approximately eighty articles and sermons published in books, journals, and encyclopedias; and some 138 book reviews. Beyond this he edited, co-edited, or co-authored five other books and translated one book from German into English. The titles of the major publications which he wrote or with which he was involved provide an excellent indication of the changes in, as well as the wide-ranging character of, Niebuhr's theological and ethical interests.

As a doctoral student at Yale University, Niebuhr produced a dissertation on *Ernst Troeltsch's Philosophy of Religion* (1924), in which he examined this early-twentieth-century German theologian's philosophy of religion from the standpoint of his theory of knowledge and his understanding of history. The problems that were central for Troeltsch, those of the historical relativity and the cultural conditionedness of all man's thought and sociality, became determinative for Niebuhr's future work. He immediately put what he had learned from Troeltsch to work in an analysis of the decisive role of social factors in the development of denominations in American religious life. The result was his first published book, *The Social Sources of Denominationalism* (1929), which brought the young theologian widespread recognition and the invitation to teach at Yale.

Already in this work Niebuhr showed some restlessness with the reigning liberal theology in America, but by the early thirties the winds of theological change blowing from continental Europe had struck with great force. Although influenced by Karl Barth's dialectical theology, Niebuhr preferred Paul Tillich's "belief-ful realism" and helped to introduce this brand of theology of culture to America by translating Tillich's *The Religious Situation* (1932). By the mid-thirties H. Richard and his brother Reinhold were spearheading the movement to recover the insights of Reformation theology for Americans and, in what is probably his strongest reaction to liberalism, Niebuhr collaborated with Wilhelm Pauck and Francis P. Miller to write a book they entitled *The Church Against the World* (1935). In a chapter called "Toward the Independence of the Church," Niebuhr pleaded for the liberation of the church from its worldly bondage to capitalism, nationalism, and humanism, and for a return to true loyalty to God.

Dissatisfaction with his earlier treatment of the development of Protestant Christianity in America soon led Niebuhr to a re-examination which, without denying the importance of social factors in forming the denominations, attempted to do justice to the theological convictions that provided the dynamic force within the Protestant movement. The result was *The Kingdom of God in America* (1937), in which he depicted the whole sweep of American church history as a movement propelled by the idea of the kingdom of God, understood initially as God's sovereignty (Puritanism), then as the reign of Christ (Evangelicalism), and finally as the kingdom on earth (Social Gospel). Continuing his effort to denote the peculiarly Christian within what appears to be a sea of historical and cultural relativism, Niebuhr next wrote what many consider to be his finest theological treatise, *The Meaning of Revelation* (1941). Revelation, he insisted, does not consist of miraculous events that any disinterested observer can see, but it involves, rather, an event in the inner history of the self which illuminates its whole history and makes it intelligible.

Although the forties witnessed a stream of significant articles from Niebuhr's pen, ten long years of international war and reconstruction were to pass before the appearance of *Christ and Culture* (1951), his best-known work. In it Niebuhr analyzed the problem of how Christians are related to their cultural setting and offered a typology covering the spectrum from total opposition to total accommodation. Niebuhr's constant engagement in the task of teaching courses in Christian ethics led him to collaborate with Professor Waldo Beach of Duke University in the editing of a sourcebook of significant readings in the field: *Christian Ethics: Sources of the Living Tradition* (1955). A revealing commentary on Niebuhr's own interests is provided by the fact that he chose to write the introductions and to select the readings for the sections on the ethics of the Bible, Martin Luther, John Calvin, and Jonathan Edwards.

Mention has already been made of the publications resulting from the study of theological education in the United States and Canada, but *The Purpose of the Church and Its Ministry* (1956) deserves to be singled out as a book containing Niebuhr's own reflections on the aim of the church, the emerging conception of the ministry, and the idea of a theological school. More sharply than in any other book Niebuhr here set forth his understanding of the nature and function of theology, which he insisted had as its object, not God in his isolation, but "God in his relations to the self with its companions, and the self with its companions in their relations to God."

In 1957 Niebuhr delivered a set of lectures on contemporary civilization at the University of Nebraska, and these were later revised and expanded to form the last book published during his lifetime, *Radical Monotheism and Western Culture* (1960), which also included four supplementary essays written at various times but pertinent to the main subject. The burden of this work is to show how radical monotheistic faith has differed from polytheistic and henotheistic faiths in the history of Western religion, politics, and science, and in no other writing does the universal outlook emerging from Niebuhr's faith appear with such clarity.

[17]

At the time of his unexpected death on July 5, 1962, H. Richard Niebuhr stood on the threshold of retirement from his academic duties at Yale and of the writing of his *magnum opus*, a systematic treatment of Christian ethics. Although denied the full fruit of thirty years' reflection on the subject, the world did receive an essay in Christian moral philosophy that can be looked upon as a kind of prolegomenon to the projected *opus*. Published posthumously as *The Responsible Self* (1963), with a preface by his son Richard and an introduction by James M. Gustafson, the volume contains the Robertson Lectures that Niebuhr delivered at the University of Glasgow in 1960 and, in an appendix, portions of his Earl Lectures at the Pacific School of Religion in 1962. In these lectures Niebuhr centered his understanding of human life around the symbol of responsibility and advocated an ethics that asked not so much about "the good" or "the right" as about "the fitting."

For almost forty years H. Richard Niebuhr carried out his ministry of writing and teaching as a servant of the church. His controlling interest was always one of church reformation, and to a remarkable degree his thought remained at the cutting edge between the Christian faith and the world of unbelief, at times calling the church to defend the substance of its faith against the world and at other times demanding that the church engage the world for the sake of its mission, but at all times keeping church and world in dialogue with one another. He was well versed not only in the theological disciplines, but also in sociology, history, and philosophy, and he brought the insights of these various disciplines to bear upon one another. He was at home in the history of Christian thought and made a special contribution to Americans by helping them to understand the importance of their own theological heritage. When all is said and done, H. Richard Niebuhr was a many-sided and gifted man, but in all that he did he intended to be nothing more than a theologian of grace,

[18]

refusing to absolutize anything finite or to replace dialectical thinking with a synthesis, but believing that God, who alone is absolute, does make himself present in our history and does forge his own synthesis.

II
Niebuhr's Thought

In his article, "Reformation: Continuing Imperative" (1960), which was Niebuhr's contribution to *The Christian Century*'s "How My Mind Has Changed" series, the seasoned theologian looked back upon thirty years' experience and concluded that his fundamental convictions about God and man had not changed since they were established during the thirties. From that time forward he was convinced of the sovereignty of God; of the lostness and sinfulness of man; and of the fact that faith in God, which brings forgiveness and justification to man, is a miraculous gift. To be sure, his theological formulations had undergone change and emphases had shifted, but this is as it should be, he explained, since theological formulations are not the basis but only the expression of faith and since they must be continually related to an ever-changing historical and cultural context.

While granting some validity to the view that in the early thirties he changed from "liberal theology" to "neo-orthodoxy" and then in the fifties from "neo-orthodoxy" in its later forms back to "liberalism," Niebuhr eschewed the use of such labels and disavowed the interpretation that is implied in this reading of his intellectual history. If affirmation of the radically historical character of human existence is a tenet of liberalism, then he had always been a liberal. Likewise, if belief in the sovereignty of God is central to orthodoxy or to neo-orthodoxy, then he had been orthodox or neo-orthodox since the early thirties. In other words, his own case can serve as a good illustration of the fallacy of using such broad and misleading categories. His own view of recent history was that the correction initiated by Karl Barth and other dialectical theologians in the twenties and early thirties was necessary in order to overcome the tendency toward a man-centered faith in cultural Protestantism, but that it became an overcorrection which threatened to turn the understanding of faith into mere assent to "right doctrine."

For his own part Niebuhr aligned himself theologically with the "great tradition" of Augustine, Thomas, Luther, Calvin, Pascal, and Edwards. Moreover, he avowed a greater kinship with "theologians of experience," such as Edwards, Schleiermacher, Coleridge, Bushnell, and Maurice, than with "theologians of doctrine," a group with whom he associated the later Barth and much of the "dogmatic biblical theology" current in 1960. He declared his conviction that the way of the future for Protestant theology should be the resumption of "the general line of march represented by the evangelical, empirical, and critical movement," and it is noteworthy that he felt he had never abandoned, although he had reworked, the religious empiricism, historism, and neo-Kantian epistemology of his liberal background.

These mature reflections of Niebuhr on his theological lineage and central convictions are helpful in providing a general orientation for his thought, although it is obvious that both matters deserve more detailed and critical attention. We turn now to an exposition of his theological and ethical thought, and if the reader is to make any judgment about what is promising in the thought of H. Richard Niebuhr, it seems imperative that a fairly well-rounded presentation be made. His thought may be likened to a cut diamond. It is all of a piece, something forged through the exertion of great pressures over a period of time. Yet it is not round and smooth like a marble, possessing the dull perfection of a sphere. Instead, it achieves its unity as well as its brilliance from its many facets, all of which are cut at odd angles but which work together to produce a single effect that is precious indeed. Such an analogy, of course, does not do justice to the fluidity and flexibility of Niebuhr's thought, but the intention is simply to underscore the desirability of examining the many facets of Niebuhr's thought in the hope that a kind of sparkling wholeness will appear. Then it may be more feasible to judge whether some facets are more significant for the future than others.

Faith, the Gods, and God

The meaning of faith is a theme that recurs time and again in the writings of H. Richard Niebuhr. Not since Wilhelm Herrmann has any theologian been so persistent in arguing that faith is to be properly understood not as *fides* but as *fiducia*, that is, not as intellectual assent to propositions or belief in certain teachings or doctrines but as personal trust or reliance on something or someone. The emphasis on faith as *fiducia*, or trust, was not only characteristic of Ritschlian theologians like Herrmann, of course, but also goes back to Schleiermacher and then especially to Luther. Niebuhr, however, believed that faith had an additional meaning that these men did not stress, but which he found in full measure in the religious philosophy of the American, Josiah Royce. Faith is trust, but at the same time it is also loyalty or *fidelitas*. For Niebuhr, no definition would suffice unless it included both these aspects. To have faith is to trust another and to be loyal to the other and to the other's cause.

Niebuhr's understanding of faith is directly related to his understanding of God, and he explored this relation between faith and God in *The Meaning of Revelation* and again in a profound essay that appeared two years later in *motive*, entitled "The Nature and Existence of God" (1943). It is interesting to note that when he included this essay as a supplement to his book, *Radical Monotheism and*

Western Culture, Niebuhr changed the title to "Faith in Gods and in God." Given his definition of faith, it is not surprising that when Niebuhr tackled the problem of God in this essay, he did not begin by raising the speculative question, "Does God exist?" but, rather, posed the subjective and personal question, "How is faith in God possible?" That is, faith is primarily interested in the character and power of God, not in his existence.

It is Niebuhr's thesis that *all* men live by faith. We experience this in everyday life as we have confidence in and rely upon other people. But beyond this, all men have what we would call religious faith, although this fact is often unrecognized because we tend to identify religion with organizations and institutions. By religious faith Niebuhr meant the faith that life is worth living, the faith in certain centers of value that bestow meaning and worth on our existence. In Niebuhr's words, ". . . no man lives without living for some purpose, for the glorification of some god, for the advancement of some cause" (RMWC, 118).* Whatever we rely upon that makes our life worth living, that is our god, so that to have faith always means to have a god. To support this view Niebuhr liked to quote Luther, who said, "Trust and faith of the heart alone make both God and idol. . . . For the two, faith and God, hold close together. Whatever than thy heart clings to . . . and relies upon, that is properly thy god" (MR, 23).

If it be true that every man relies upon some god to make his life worthwhile, then the natural religion of man is polytheism. Men have many gods, concluded Niebuhr, and there is actually no such thing as atheism, even though many profess it. The being to which we are most commonly devoted, of course, is our own self, and yet no man can live entirely for his own sake. We make gods out of our children, our homes, our country, our ideologies, our churches, our

*See page 116 for the key to abbreviations referring to Niebuhr's writings.

moral values, art, sex, and so on—whatever we depend on to deliver our lives from meaninglessness and nothingness. The problem that Niebuhr sees in this is that none of our gods, none of our centers of value, exists universally or can be object of a universal faith. Because they are finite in time and in space, our gods can only make finite claims on us and can guarantee meaning to our lives only for a time. The result is inevitable conflict, both within ourselves and within society, and this is what Niebuhr refers to as the tragedy of our religion. But the tragedy involves more than internal and social division and the attendant frustration of being unable to integrate our gods into some great pantheon. The greater tragedy, declared Niebuhr, is "the twilight of the gods," the discovery that none of the beings on which we rely to give content and meaning to our lives is able to supply this continuously. Our causes, our great social movements, our ideals, our empires and cities—all of these pass away, and at the end nothing is able to save us from the void of meaninglessness.

What is this "void" that is the enemy of all our causes, the opponent of all our gods? Niebuhr answered in these words:

> We may call it the nature of things, we may call it fate, we may call it reality. But by whatever name we call it, this law of things, this reality, this way things are, is something with which we all must reckon. We may not be able to give a name to it, calling it only the "void" out of which everything comes and to which everything returns, though that is also a name. But it is there—the last shadowy and vague reality, the secret of existence by which things come into being, are what they are, and pass away. Against it there is no defense (RMWC, 122).

It was Niebuhr's conviction that this void, this reality in which we live and move and have our being, is God and that somehow this enemy of our gods, this last power, comes to be known and counted upon as our friend. Through a strange happening we come to attach our faith, hope, and love to this One who is the source of all and the slayer of all.

In Niebuhr's estimation no one has expressed what is involved here better than Alfred North Whitehead, when he said that religion "is transition from God the void to God the enemy, and from God the enemy to God the companion."1 * But how does this transition ever come about? How is such a faith possible? What causes this "happening"? Much is involved, because the whole man is involved. This faith, stressed Niebuhr, comes not without a kind of sober despair that has faced the reality of the death of all things and the endlessness of the creative process, not without the struggle of man's reason to make sense out of life, not without the frustrating experience of inner division and of social catastrophe, not without the operation of something like spiritual intuition or creative insight, and not without moral struggle over our own unworthiness. But although all these elements are involved, there is yet another one, which for Niebuhr is crucial, namely, "the concrete meeting with other men who have received this faith, and the concrete meeting with Jesus Christ" (RMWC, 124). This brings us to Niebuhr's understanding of revelation.

Revelation and History

Niebuhr cannot speak of revelation apart from history. Yet the relation between revelation and history is extraordinarily complex, and it is with this complexity that Niebuhr wrestles in *The Meaning of Revelation*, the book which in 1941 Paul Tillich called "*the* introduction into existential thinking in present American theology."2 In dealing with revelation and faith, Niebuhr resolutely adopted the historical point of view and reminded his readers that the Christian community had been most vigorous when it spoke in confessional terms about the events that had happened to it in its history. For example, the preaching of the early church was not an argument for the existence of God but a recital of the great events connected with the historical appearance of Jesus Christ and a con-

*Superior figures refer to the Notes at the end of the text.

fession of what had happened to the community of disciples. Niebuhr was convinced that the church today could do no better than follow the historical method of the New Testament and that it was a grave error to suppose that one could substitute for this an approach based on metaphysics or an abstract system of morality.

Because we are historical beings, everything must be seen through the medium of our history. In Niebuhr's vivid words: "We are in history as the fish is in water and what we mean by the revelation of God can be indicated only as we point through the medium in which we live" (MR, 48). Nature does not point us to God unless it is interpreted through our history and faith, and the same is true of Scripture. Unless those who read it share in the same spiritual history as those who recorded it, the Bible is not revelation. Even a historical Jesus cannot be known, said Niebuhr, except through the history and with the history of the community that loved and worshiped him. Individualists have attempted to circumvent the historical point of view by identifying revelation with events that occur in their private, inner life or with an inner moral imperative, but Niebuhr pointed out that the "inner light" is identified with "Christ," a word that comes out of social history, and that moral imperatives for the Christian can have no meaning or content unless these are derived from the history of our Lord. Not even the mystic can escape history.

For Niebuhr the crucial question is: How can revelation mean both history and God? Must not what we see from the historical point of view and what we believe in be two different things? To the objective historian is there anything unique about Jesus, except the uniqueness that is characteristic of every event in time? And if we say that revelation means history, does this imply that faith is attached to the occurrence of certain divine events in the past, and if so, is this not a denial of faith in a living God who is active here and now? In his attempt to solve these

[26]

problems Niebuhr distinguished between two types of
history. Using the Kantian distinction between the theoretical reason and the practical reason as a basis, he differ-
entiated between the external history that is seen and the
internal history that is lived.

External history is the realm of theoretical reason, where
events in history are observed from without as objectively
and disinterestedly as possible. Here the approach is impersonal, the primary concern is with objects, and the result is
descriptive knowledge. On the other hand, internal history
is the realm of practical reason, where the concern is not
with detached observation but with the meaning of events
for one's life. One participates in this history and thus sees
everything from the inside. The approach is personal, the
concern is with subjects, and the result is normative
knowledge. Niebuhr pointed to still further differences. In
external history the value of an event is measured by its
valency or strength, time is measured serially, and society is
considered an association of individuals related solely by
external bonds. On the contrary, in internal history, value
is measured by its worth for selves, time is a duration in
which both past and future are present as memory and
potentiality, and society is a community of selves who are
personally and internally related. Finally, Niebuhr related
the two kinds of history to a distinction made famous by
Martin Buber: outer history involves an I-It relationship,
inner history an I-Thou relationship.

How does the differentiation between outer and inner
history help Niebuhr to solve the problem of how revelation can mean both history and God? First of all, it allows
him to affirm that revelation really takes place in history
and yet at the same time to deny that revelation is
identifiable with miraculous events visible to any detached
observer. But on the other hand, it makes possible an
understanding of how events that are revelatory in our
history can yet be analyzed disinterestedly by an observer.
When the chips are down, Niebuhr locates the revelation of

God primarily in internal history, but he nevertheless understood the significance of the paradoxical relationship between internal and external history for the Christian community. Even though this community begins with an internal knowledge of its destiny, it must necessarily accept the external views others have of it and, indeed, often profits from external criticism. Furthermore, Niebuhr pointed out that just because the Christian community remembers the revelatory moment in its own history, it must regard all events as the workings of the God who reveals himself, even though it can view most of these events only externally. Finally, Niebuhr was convinced that the church must try to achieve an external view of itself, not only because its inner life is inevitably embodied in outer history but also because it is obliged to attempt to see his own history as God sees it.

As was indicated above, for Niebuhr the revelatory event has its primary location in inner history. Of course, not all of inner history is revelation, but only one part—and that not arbitrarily chosen by man but given him by the grace of God. Niebuhr explained the meaning of revelation in these words:

Revelation means for us that part of our inner history which illuminates the rest of it and which is itself intelligible. Sometimes when we read a difficult book, seeking to follow a complicated argument, we come across a luminous sentence from which we can go forward and backward and so attain some understanding of the whole. Revelation is like that. In his *Religion in the Making* Professor Whitehead has written such illuminating sentences and one of them is this: "Rational religion appeals to the direct intuition of special occasions, and to the elucidatory power of its concepts for all occasions." The special occasion to which we appeal in the Christian church is called Jesus Christ, in whom we see the righteousness of God, his power and wisdom. But from that special occasion we also derive the concepts which make possible the elucidation of all the events in our history. Revelation means this intelligible event which makes all other events intelligible (MR, 93).

[28]

Obviously Niebuhr believed that Jesus Christ, the "occasion" of Christian revelation, was a real man who lived in Palestine almost two milleniums ago, who "suffered under Pontius Pilate, was crucified, dead, and buried." His history can be observed externally, but only when through faith we participate in that history does he become God's self-revelation to us.

Did Niebuhr's emphasis on internal history lead him to a subjectivism in which the "object" of revelation is lost? Niebuhr did not think so. He affirmed historical relativism (or better: historical relationism) in the sense that man is in time and time is in him. Man can gain no vantage point outside history, but must conceive all things as temporal and historical and must think as one conditioned by the time in which he lives. Nevertheless, this does not imply subjectivism, nor lead to skepticism. "It is not evident," he stated, "that the man who is forced to confess that his view of things is conditioned by the standpoint he occupies must doubt the reality of what he sees. It is not apparent . . . that one who understands how all his experience is historically mediated must believe that nothing is mediated through history" (MR, 18f.). Furthermore, Niebuhr stressed that the revelation perceived in the event of faith is not merely private but is corroborated socially. Others experience the same reality.

In summary, Niebuhr attempted in his historical method to recognize the objectivity of the reality encountered in the event of revelation but at the same time to do justice to the relativity of all historical knowledge. Two implications of this approach should be emphasized at this time. First, for Niebuhr theology is confessional rather than apologetic in character. He did not think Christianity should try to prove its superiority; in fact, he considered self-defense to be the most prevalent source of error in all thinking. Christians are called to testify to their faith in God, but they do so from their relative historical standpoint. They never possess revelation; they may possess the memory of Jesus Christ, but revelation itself is always an event.

Second, Christian thinking is confined primarily to the realm of the practical reason or, better, the historical reason. Theology is concerned with the moral and religious issues of life where value judgments must be made, and here Niebuhr, following Pascal, emphasized that the reasons of the heart rather than the reasons of the head hold sway. In this realm images and symbols are preferred to the rational concepts of theoretical reason. In saying this Niebuhr did not mean that revelation, or thinking based on revelation, is irrational. Rather, he wished merely to insist that the conceptual patterns employed by theoretical reason to understand the behavior of things are unsuitable for use in the personal sphere of inner history.

The God of Revelation

H. Richard Niebuhr was a strictly theocentric thinker. We have already learned of his conviction that no one can escape God. Even though man may not recognize God, he inevitably encounters him as the "void" and the enemy of the lesser gods. According to Niebuhr there are no real atheists, for we all place our faith in the finite gods that seem to make our lives worth living. We naturally tend to be polytheists, but our diverse loyalties lead to the problem of inner personal conflict and outward social disruption. Moreover, our gods cannot stand the pace of time and in the end fail us. Both we and our gods meet in history a final power that opposes and slays. For Niebuhr this void, this enemy, is God, who is always present in history. We find this conviction expressed quite early in Niebuhr's writings. An excellent example is found in an article he directed to his brother Reinhold in 1932, entitled "The Only Way into the Kingdom of God":

> For my brother God is outside the historical processes, so much so that he charges me with faith in a miracle-working deity which

interferes occasionally, sometimes brutally, sometimes redemptively, in this history. But God, I believe, is always in history; he is the structure in things, the source of all meaning, the "I am that I am," that which is that it is. He is the rock against which we beat in vain, that which bruises and overwhelms us when we seek to impose our wishes, contrary to his, upon him. That structure of the universe, that will of God, can no more be said to interfere brutally in history than the violated laws of my organism can be said to interfere brutally with my life if they make me pay the cost of my violation. [3]

For Niebuhr, then, God is the ultimate reality present in all history, the great Rock on which our idolatries founder. Men have presentiments of his presence, vague notions of this enemy who brings all to nought. Niebuhr could speak of a kind of natural knowledge of deity, very weak and inadequate and yet seemingly necessary, since our confession of faith in the revealed God implies some previous knowledge of what deity is and since even apart from revelation we can speak about God with members of non-Christian communities. But the crucial question is how one moves from this "natural knowledge" to knowledge of the revealed God. How does one move from God the enemy to God the companion and friend? What brings about the change from faith in the many gods to faith in the One? Niebuhr answers these questions by pointing to the revelation of God in Jesus Christ.

Through Jesus Christ, through his life, death, and resurrection, God has revealed himself. This is the affirmation of the Christian community, and it was Niebuhr's affirmation. It is this revelation that elicits, nay, compels, faith in God. Niebuhr never ceased to be amazed at the occurrence of faith, which he could only interpret as a miraculous gift. He believed that no man could will Christian faith for himself. Just as there is no continuous movement from the knowledge of theoretical reason to the knowledge of practical reason, there is none from an objective inquiry into the life of Jesus to a knowledge of him as the Christ who is the Lord or from a natural knowledge of God to the

[31]

knowledge of God who reveals himself in Christ. Involved in Christian faith is a decision of the self, a revolution of the mind, a leap of faith, but the possibility for this is given in the prior action of God. We know God only because he first knows us.

Although Niebuhr could speak of revelation as a rational event in the sense that it illuminates and makes intelligible the whole of our history, he also admitted that the faith in God that comes through the history of Jesus Christ involves what can only seem absurd to our reason. The absurd thing is that we become convinced that the final power, the slayer, is the life-giver, a trustworthy friend. Niebuhr explained it this way:

> What is the absurd thing that comes into our moral history as existential selves, but the conviction, mediated by a life, a death, and a miracle beyond understanding, that the source and ground and government and end of all things—the power we (in our distrust and disloyalty) call fate and chance—is faithful, utterly trustworthy, utterly loyal to all that issues from it? . . . To metaphysical thinking the irrational thing is the incarnation of the infinite, the temporalizing of the absolute. But this is not the absurdity to our existential, subjective, decision-making thought. What is irrational here is the creation of faith in the faithfulness of God by the crucifixion, the betrayal of Jesus Christ, who was utterly loyal to Him. (CC, 254).

The surd is that this man who was faithful and loyal to God should come to this shameful end, like the rest of us, and yet, as a consequence, faith in the God of his faith is called forth in us. Here the resurrection of Jesus Christ becomes crucial for Niebuhr. The man of faith becomes convinced that God is faithful, that he kept faith with Jesus Christ, that Christ is risen from the dead, "that as the Power is faithful so Christ's faithfulness is powerful; that we can say 'Our Father' to that which has elected us to live, to die, and to inherit life beyond life" (CC, 255). Niebuhr can even say that "unless there enters into our existence the demonstration, as it were, of the loyalty of the Lord of Heaven and earth to this One who was so loyal to Him and so loyal to his fellow man we can't believe in God."[4]

It was Niebuhr's conviction that the revelation of God in Jesus Christ is an event in our history which revolutionizes our human religion, which is usually polytheistic (faith in many gods) and at best henotheistic (faith in one god among many). Faith in the many is converted into faith in the One who is beyond the many but who acts in and through all things. Thus Christian faith is radically monotheistic. In a world in which everything is relative to history there is only one Absolute to which everything historical is related, and that Absolute is God. Niebuhr understood the revelation of God in Christ to introduce a permanent revolution in our religious life whereby our religious beliefs and conduct are continually transformed through repentance and new faith.

In his self-revelation who does God reveal himself to be? We have seen that for Niebuhr God is One, but much more is involved in a Christian understanding of God than the principle of unity. Indeed, Niebuhr has an unusually rich conception of God which includes an element of universality as well as an element of redemption. In order to differentiate these two elements which in fact are inseparable, he often speaks of God as "God-in-Christ" (accenting the universal) and "Christ-in-God" (accenting the redemptive). On the one hand, God is Being Itself, the Source and Center of all being, the Universal One who is beyond the many but from whom the many derive their being and, by participation, in whom they all exist. He is the Ground of Being, the Determiner of destiny. On the other hand, in Jesus Christ God makes himself known as First Person, as an "I" who is faithful and loving as only selves are faithful and loving. He is a Father who cares for his children, who hears and answers prayer, who enters into covenant relationships. In the event of revelation God discloses himself to be an infinite person who knows us from beginning to end, who is our author, judge, and only savior. It is he who raised Jesus from the dead, the Lord of both life and death. In short, God is the Creator and Sustainer of all that is, the Judge and Redeemer of his creature man.

For Niebuhr, God is not only the principle of unity and the principle of being, but also the principle of value. Indeed, he emphasized that for the radical monotheist the center of value is the principle of Being Itself. As the One who is the source and only savior of the many beings, God is the value-center who bestows value on beings. The consequences of this are twofold. In the first place, every existent is to be revered because it has received value from God. Whether man or animal, animate or inanimate, each finite being should be reverenced as valuable because of its relation to God, who is infinite and absolute. Thus Niebuhr can affirm that "whatever is, is good." The second consequence, however, is the utter centrality of God as the ultimate value-giver. To make anything less than God the absolute or the center of value is for Niebuhr the essence of sin and idolatry. Thus he can affirm the First Commandment as another motto of radical monotheism: "I am the Lord thy God; thou shalt have no other gods before me."

Niebuhr did not believe that the church could speak of God's *aseity*, that is, his being by and for himself. The God who reveals himself and is known to the church is not an isolated God, but the God who is intimately related to the whole of creation. Niebuhr particularly stressed that men never know God except in relation to themselves and to their neighbors. The object of theological thinking is never God-in-himself but "God in relation to self and neighbor, and self and neighbor in relation to God" (PCM, 113). Because he believed that the fundamental relation of all men is to God and that every relationship is historically qualified, Niebuhr could speak of a Christian relation to God but not of a Christian God. He explained his position in this way: "I cannot presume to think as a Jew or a Mohammedan would think about God, though I recognize

[34]

that they are thinking about the same God about whom I think. ... There is no such being, or source of being, surely, as a Christian God (though there may be Christian idols); but there is a Christian relation to God and I cannot abstract from that, as no Jew or Mohammedan can abstract from a Jewish or Muslim relation" (RS, 45).

In *The Meaning of Revelation* Niebuhr endeavored to indicate something of the revolution of man's natural knowledge of God that takes place through the revelation of God in Jesus Christ. He referred specifically to our ideas about divine unity, power, and goodness. We tend to think of God, he said, as one unconditioned being beyond the many conditioned beings among which we live, "the apex of a pyramid that we build on earthly foundations according to our own design" (MR, 184). But the Father of our Lord Jesus Christ met us "not as the one beyond the many but as the one who acts in and through all things, not as the unconditioned but as the conditioner. The oneness of the person was the oneness of a will directed towards unity of all things in our world" (MR, 183). Our life comes to us through him, for in every event we meet God and in every moment we must try to think his thoughts after him. Niebuhr believed that the traditional doctrine of the Trinity was an attempt to understand the unity of God, although he did not think it was an altogether satisfactory or final formulation of the truth that the God who comes to man in Jesus Christ and the God of our religious imagination is one.

Just as revelation requires us to make a new beginning in our thought about God's oneness, it also makes us rethink our ideas about the power of deity. Niebuhr reminds us that we all know what it means to be strong in the world, and we expect God's power to be no less than worldly power. Yet God's power is made manifest in the weakness of Jesus. His meek and humble life ended in death, but death was not the last reality. Through death the life of Jesus was raised to power; through him it was shown that there is a power greater than the power of death. "We see the power of God over the strong of earth," declared Niebuhr, "made evident not in the fact that he slays them, but in his making the spirit of the slain Jesus unconquerable. ... His power is made perfect in weakness and he exercises sovereignty more through crosses than through thrones" (MR, 187).

It is the natural belief of the human community that deity must not only be powerful, but must also be good. Without the value of goodness God could not command loyalty. But Niebuhr pointed out that the goodness we expect of deity is both intrinsic and instrumental. That is, in our natural state of polytheism we tend to direct our worship to one set of beings and to direct our prayers to another. "We adore and worship that for the sake of which we live; we pray to that which is able to preserve the beings we adore. If deity is one it needs to combine with power an adorable and a ministering goodness" (MR, 188). Thus we enter the moment of revelation with fairly definite ideas about the good we seek to love, but the good that finds us in revelation is beyond our expectations and puts us to shame. Niebuhr speaks of the goodness of the Father of Jesus Christ as the "simple everyday goodness of love," the value belonging to a person rather than existing in an idea or pattern. It is the goodness that exists as pure activity, "goodness that empties itself, and makes itself of no reputation, a goodness that is all outgoing, reserving nothing for itself, yet having all things" (MR, 190). In the face of such a goodness Niebuhr was sure that we must rethink all our definitions of deity and convert all our worship and our prayers. The good does not define God, but God defines the good.

We have seen, then, that in Niebuhr's view the God of revelation is the God of history who is actively present in each and every event and yet is One, who is Being and yet Person, whose power is good and whose goodness is powerful. He affirmed, on the one hand, that the valuing,

[36]

saving power in the world is the principle of being itself, and, on the other hand, that the principle of being gives and maintains and re-establishes worth. Niebuhr spoke as a Christian for whom Jesus Christ is the revelation of God, although he spoke only confessionally and did not deny the possibility that God reveals himself in other ways. He once wrote: "I do not have the evidence which allows me to say that the miracle of faith in God is worked only by Jesus Christ and that it is never given to men outside the sphere of his working, though I may say that where I note its presence I posit the presence also of something like Jesus Christ."[5]

Niebuhr's understanding of God as the principle of unity, being, and value led him to advocate a radical monotheism, but at the same time he espoused a Trinitarian view of God. Although he never developed his own doctrine of the Trinity and gave many indications that the doctrine of the fourth century would not suffice for our day, he nevertheless wanted to be understood as a Trinitarian. Perhaps no better indication of this is afforded than the following statement from an article entitled "An Attempt at a Theological Analysis of Missionary Motivation," which he wrote in 1951:

> The theological standpoint from which I shall endeavor to view these [missionary] motives is Trinitarian, that is to say, it is neither Christocentric, nor spiritualistic, nor creativistic, but all of these at once. In this sense it seeks to be theocentric. I seek to understand as one who believes in God, the Father, Almighty Creator of heaven and earth and in Jesus Christ his Son, who for us men and our salvation was incarnate, was crucified, raised from the dead and reigns with the Father as one God, and in the Holy Spirit who proceeds from the Father and the Son (from the Father as much as from the Son), and who is the immanent divine principle not only in the church but in the world created and governed by God.[6]

This statement clearly shows Niebuhr's desire to be a *theo*-centric thinker and his suspicion of any theology which placed too much emphasis on any one of the "persons" of the Trinity. He was particularly disturbed by the tendency in modern theology to equate theology with Christology, which he considered to be a new unitarianism of the second person of the Trinity. In fact, he stated that in his own confession of faith, as in that of many men he knew, "the expression of trust in God and vow of loyalty to him comes before the acknowledgement of Christ's lordship."7

This attitude of Niebuhr's toward the Trinitarian view of God and the problem of unitarianism is foreshadowed in an article he published in 1946 on "The Doctrine of the Trinity and the Unity of the Church." In it he pointed out that one can approach the doctrine of the Trinity from various points of view. For instance, one can begin with man's enduring crisis as he wrestles with the existential problem of God and of his relation to God. This problem inevitably leads to questions about the deity of the Creator of nature (of his goodness), the deity of Jesus Christ (of his power), and the deity of the Spirit (whether among all the spirits there is a Holy Spirit). However, Niebuhr chose to approach the question of the Trinity from the standpoint of ecumenical theology, his interest being to show how the doctrine of the Trinity can serve as a formulation of the *whole* church's faith in God in distinction from the partial faiths and partial formulations.

The difficulty Niebuhr saw with the Trinitarian understanding of God was not that Christianity became a polytheism with three gods (tritheism), but that it was more often a loose association of three unitarian religions. Those who are more philosophically oriented and who are primarily interested in natural theology tend to develop a unitarianism of the Creator, who is considered to be the First Cause and the Great Designer of heaven and earth. Where interest is not so much in philosophical explanations or in man's place in nature but in personal salvation, a unitarianism of the Son tends to emerge. Christ is the Lord who brings redemption from sin, and worship is concentrated on him. Finally, a unitarianism of the Spirit arises when the focus of interest is not on the Being beyond nature nor on the Redeemer in history but on the divine reality found in man's inner life, in his reason or feeling or conscience or self-consciousness. In this case, explained Niebuhr, it is not that God is spirit but that spirit is God, so that in the direct spiritual awareness of religious experience man is in touch with God.

Niebuhr's chief concern in this article was to disclose the inadequacies of the three unitarianisms and to show how they are actually interdependent. Each unitarianism arises in part as a protest against an overemphasis of the deity of one of the other persons of the Trinity. Unitarianism of the Creator is a protest against the exclusive reliance on Scripture for the knowledge of God or the exclusive worship of the Christ of Scripture. In the case of Deism it was a protest against the overenthusiasm of the spiritualists. Unitarianism of the Son is a protest against exclusive concern with the Creator or with rational knowledge as the way to faith or with the teachings about the goodness of man's created nature. Unitarianism of the Spirit is a protest against exclusive concern with the rational knowledge of God as known in nature or with the historical knowledge of God as known in history. Thus the three unitarianisms are historically and psychologically interrelated, but Niebuhr also argued that they are logically interrelated, since each form of unitarianism depends on the convictions represented in the other forms and since each form tends to pass over into the others.

The interrelationships are fairly easy for Niebuhr to demonstrate. The Christian calls the Creator of nature the Father of Jesus Christ; fatherhood implies sonship, so the God of nature is related to Jesus Christ the Son. Reasoning about nature is often connected with religious experience, so that the Creator is related to the Spirit within man. Furthermore, no one who raises the question of Christ's power can escape the question of his relation to the

Creator, just as no one can maintain a religious relationship to Jesus Christ without recourse to spiritual experience. Finally, spiritual life seems unreal unless man can understand nature itself as a manifestation of Spirit, and the spiritualist has no way to "test the spirit" except by turning to the Son. Niebuhr concluded that none of the unitarianisms can stand alone, and for no other reason than this the church would have to formulate a doctrine of the Trinity. Actually, the Trinitarian doctrine is able to represent the wholeness of the church by stating what is implicit in the faith and knowledge of all its parts (its unitarianisms) though it is not explicit in any one of them. Niebuhr indicated that this ecumenical approach to the doctrine would include rather than exclude the heretics, but would at the same time try to correct the overemphases found in the three unitarianisms. The testimony of the *whole* church would be this: God is one and there is but one God, but God reveals himself to be simultaneously Father, Son, and Holy Spirit.

We have discussed many aspects of Niebuhr's understanding of God, but in the end there was one note which he accented above all others and which seemed to sum up everything he wanted to affirm about God. That note was "the sovereignty of God." Above all else, Niebuhr believed that God is sovereign. In 1960 he reflected on what this conviction had meant in his own history:

> The thirties were for me as for many of my generation in the church the decisive period in the formation of basic personal convictions and in the establishment of theological formulations of those convictions. The fundamental certainty given to me then (sad to say, not in such a way that my unconscious as well as conscious mind has been wholly permeated by it) was that of God's sovereignty. My fundamental break with the so-called liberal or empirical theology was not due to the fact that it emphasized human sovereignty; to interpret it in that way is to falsify it in unjustifiable fashion. It was rather due to the fact that it defined God primarily in value-terms, as the good, believing that good could be defined apart from God. And now I came to understand

[40]

that unless being itself, the constitution of things, the One beyond all the many, the ground of my being and of all being, the ground of its "that-ness" and its "so-ness," was trustworthy—could be counted on by what had proceeded from it—I had no God at all. The change was not a change of definition of God but of personal relations to my world and the ground of the world, to the givenness of life, history, myself.[8]

It would be wrong to assume that the understanding of God's sovereignty was mediated to Niebuhr solely by the dialectical theologians of Europe. Although their focus on the Bible and the theology of the Reformers was an influence, much more important in Niebuhr's developing thought was what he learned from his study of the history of theology in America. The results of his research were published in *The Kingdom of God in America* (1937), and the thesis of this book is that the idea of the kingdom of God had been the dominant idea in the development of American Christianity, even though the idea had not always meant the same thing. "American Christianity and American culture cannot be understood at all," he declared, "save on the basis of faith in a sovereign, living, loving God" (KGA, xiv).

Niebuhr traced the meaning of the kingdom of God in America from seventeenth-century Puritanism, when it meant the sovereignty of God, through eighteenth-century Evangelicalism, when the meaning changed to the reign of Christ, to nineteenth-century Revivalism, with its emphasis on hope for the coming kingdom. The end of the nineteenth century saw the rise of Liberalism and the Social Gospel, in which the hope was understood less in terms of heavenly bliss and more in terms of an evolutionary transformation of life on earth. In all periods Christianity was understood as a dynamic movement in which God was taking the primary initiative, and the understanding of Christianity as a movement rather than an organization or institution became fundamental for Niebuhr.

Although certain elements of the meaning of the kingdom

of God in each period were congenial to Niebuhr's own theology, he basically accepted the Calvinist-Puritan view of the kingdom as the sovereign reign of God in all its nearness, absoluteness, and immediacy. God's sovereignty is not something to be established or something that came into the world from without, but it is the rule that has been established from eternity and needs only to be obeyed. Since God is sovereign, all human powers are limited. God's sovereignty is universal in extent and the basic quality of his rule is mercy and love. This is revealed in unparalleled fashion in Jesus Christ, in whom we see God's faithfulness and his will to redeem. Niebuhr did not follow the way of many Calvinists and Puritans in limiting God's redemptive will to a certain number of the elect. For him sovereignty meant that the cause of God was universal creation and universal redemption.[9]

From Evangelicalism, Niebuhr accepted the view of Christianity as a revolutionary movement begun and continued by God's acting in history. It presupposes man's bondage to sin and his need to be reborn and reconciled to Being, to the divine reality which man can but consider his enemy so long as he is intent on promoting his own will and life. Niebuhr could not accept the individualistic orientation of much of the Evangelical-Revivalist movement, however, and it was in its recognition of the social character of the kingdom of God that he saw the strength of Liberalism. The problem with Liberalism was that it no longer knew of the hard transition from God the void to God the enemy and from God the enemy to God the companion, but instead began and ended with the companion. No reconciliation to the divine sovereign was necessary, and thus the reign of Christ involved no revolutionary events in history or in the life of individuals. Reflecting on the naïve optimism of Liberalism, Niebuhr wrote what is probably his best-known sentence: "A God without wrath brought men without sin into a kingdom

[42]

without judgment through the ministrations of a Christ without a cross" (KGA, 193).

A final characteristic of God which is important for Niebuhr came from his study of the development of Christianity in America. God is not only sovereign but he is a covenanting God. Side by side with the idea of the kingdom of God in America stood the idea of the covenant, and it was Niebuhr's conviction that the covenant idea was the fundamental, though not the exclusive, pattern that guided men in the period when American democracy was formed. The ordering principle in God's kingdom is his promise or covenant, and the basic characteristic of the King is that he is faithful in keeping his promise. His administration of his kingdom is reliable, his laws can be known by patient inquiry, and their execution can be counted on. On the other hand, the subjects who live in his covenant society are called upon to enter into the covenant relationship with the King and with each other, achieving the maturity of full citizenship, accepting the laws as their own, and helping in the administration of the commonwealth. As is evident in his article on "The Idea of Covenant and American Democracy" (1954), the covenant idea of a moral society which places man's will at the center of his being was not only important for the development of democracy in America, but was crucial for Niebuhr's understanding of the world in which we live—before God.

Man's Sin and God's Grace

We have seen that for Niebuhr the proper correlate to the sovereignty of God is the faith of man. Man is that creature who is meant to respond to God in a covenant relationship of trust and loyalty. To be in a right relationship with God is to trust and to rely on him as a person

[43]

and to be loyal to his cause, which is the universal realm of being. It is to respond in every event in loyalty and confidence to the One who is present in all events. The human problem, as Niebuhr saw it, arises from the fact that man, who is created "good," perverts his own being by placing his trust in something less than God and thus enters into a rebellious relationship with His Creator. To be sure, whatever is, is good; but whatever is, is not necessarily right! Man in his sin still has faith, but his faith is in the lesser gods of the world. As a result his created nature is infected and warped by sin. Niebuhr described what happens in these words:

> The fundamental perversion of the movement of the self toward the Transcendent One has issued and issues in the misdirection, the twisting, the mark-missing of its manifold movements toward the finite. It is attracted in its religious motivation toward gods that are not good; it inverts upon itself the love that is true when it moves toward the neighbor; it moves in flight from that which does not threaten and is aggressive toward that which it ought to love. The fear of death inhibits it in its activity on the one hand, and on the other gives unnatural urgency to its desire for recognition and to its need for self-assurance. [10]

Niebuhr's most extensive discussion of the problem of sin was in an article entitled "Man the Sinner," which he published in 1935. In it he advocated what he considered to be the Christian view that all men are sinners and contrasted this "realistic" view of evil with the notion that evil is concentrated in certain individuals or classes or the romantic belief that men are good whereas institutions are bad or, finally, the view that evil represents merely the imperfection of a race that is undergoing gradual evolution, a kind of cultural lag or ignorance attributable to the race's immaturity. Niebuhr admitted that on the surface the Christian view seems more pessimistic than the others but declared that in fact it is basically more optimistic. Why? Because, said Niebuhr, the presupposition of the Christian doctrine of sin is the doctrine of creation, which teaches that man's basic nature, though perverted and obscured, is perfect. Moreover, this perfection is not something to be achieved in the far-distant future but is the underlying datum of life.

The essence of sin for Niebuhr is disloyalty to God. By disloyalty he did not mean simply the absence of loyalty but false loyalty. Instead of trusting in God and being loyal to him and his cause, man absolutizes something relative and attaches his loyalty to finite deities. Niebuhr was careful to differentiate this understanding of sin from several views which he considered to be erroneous. First, to say that man is a sinner is not the equivalent of saying that he is morally bad. Moral judgments are relative judgments that do not get to the heart of the meaning of sin, which is a religious category having to do with one's standing before God.

Second, to say that man is a sinner does not mean that he is occasionally disloyal to God or that he is disloyal only as he consciously chooses to be disloyal. The requirement of conscious, willing choice is advocated by those who stress man's accountability for sin, but in Niebuhr's opinion this whole discussion is beside the point. Christianity is not primarily concerned with the question of assessing the blame but with the fact and the cure. But even more important, this "free-will" understanding of sin rests on a highly dubious doctrine of human freedom. The starting point for the doctrine of sin, he explained, is man's dependence, not his freedom. The notion of freedom can only account for the fact that man can be and is disloyal, not for the fact that he ought to be loyal. What is important is not so much that man feel a sense of guilt, but that he come to see his disloyalty to God, his false loyalty to the gods of the world, and the ensuing consequence. Finally, even though he affirmed the Christian view that every man is a sinner, Niebuhr was opposed to making this into a general law. He believed that we should begin, not with "universal man" or with a doctrine of original sin, but with self-observation, such introspection being supported by individual and social psychology as well as by history.

What are the consequences of sin? What happens to man in his lostness? First of all, it is obvious that the sinner has a false and distorted image of himself and his world. In *The Meaning of Revelation* Niebuhr refers to "the evil imaginations of the heart" (pp. 99ff.), by which he meant those distorted and false images and myths that inhabit the self-centered and animistic world of sin. The evil of these imaginations is seen in their destructive consequences to selves and communities. We attribute every sorrow we experience to the pride of others or the inadequacy of ourselves, we imagine that whole nations or races are depraved, we have exalted images of ourselves, we attempt to use impersonal models to deal with personal affairs, and so on. Both personal and social life are afflicted by the evil imagination, and the result is error, superstition, disunity, disorder, and rationalizations of every sort. Man is inhuman to his fellow man, cruel to beasts, greedy for more than his share of earth's goods; he abuses sex, exploits nature, and commercially profanes creation. The list of offenses is endless, but it all adds up to the loss of self-integrity and to a life of irresponsibility to God and to one's neighbor. Moreover, the sinner's loyalty to his finite gods leads inevitably to increasing anxiety, defensiveness, and rebellion against God, who, to be sure, is still present to him in his sin but who is now present as his enemy.

The predicament of the sinner is nowhere more evident than in his impotence to save himself from his predicament. Niebuhr explained the problem in this way: the will of man is always committed, either to God or to one of the false gods; when man has committed his will in loyalty to a false god, he can no longer transfer his loyalty by an exercise of the will, since the will is the locus of his problem. How, then, does the sinner ever come to faith in God? We have already heard Niebuhr's answer: the miracle of faith is made possible by the self-revelation of God. Thus begins the process of conversion, *metanoia,* the permanent revolution that continues into eternity. But how does revelation take place? It happens at the initiative of God, and as a Christian Niebuhr confessed that it happens in connection with the history of Jesus Christ. This is not only his testimony but the testimony of the whole church.

This brings us to the question of Niebuhr's understanding of Jesus Christ. Who is he, and what has he accomplished? When we remember Niebuhr's commitment to the historical method, we should not be surprised by his avoidance of speculative doctrines about the person and work of Christ, such as the idea of Christ's pre-existence. We have also learned of his aversion to any "unitarianism of the Son" and his steadfast refusal to reduce theology to Christology. Yet as a Christian believer he confessed that he was a follower of Jesus Christ, that his way of thinking had been decisively modified by Christ's presence in history, that his relation to God had been deeply conditioned by Christ's presence in history, and that he identified himself whole-heartedly with Christ's cause, namely, the reconciliation of man to God (RS, 43). However, rather than defining a Christian as "a believer in Jesus Christ" or "a follower of Jesus Christ" Niebuhr thought he "might more adequately be described as one who counts himself as belonging to that community of men for whom Jesus Christ—his life, words, deeds, and destiny—is of supreme importance as the key to the understanding of themselves and their world, the main source of the knowledge of God and man, good and evil, the constant companion of the conscience, and the expected deliverer from evil" (CC, 11).

Niebuhr recognized that Christ is interpreted in a variety of ways in Christianity. Some see him as a great teacher and lawgiver, others as the revelation of God through whom new life is bestowed, and still others as the founder of a new community. However, Niebuhr stressed that, regardless of the variety, all interpretations attain a fundamental unity through the fact that they refer to the one Jesus Christ of the New Testament, who is a definite person with a definite character, definite teachings, and a definite fate. This Christ is in our history and is one and the same, whether he appears as a man of flesh and blood or as the risen Lord. There are two reasons, explained Niebuhr, why there are so many different definitions of the essence of Jesus Christ by those who recognize him as their authority. On the one hand, it is impossible to do justice to a person by means of concepts and propositions, and, on the other, everything said about this person is relative to the describer's particular standpoint in church, history, and culture. In spite of the inadequacies, however, descriptions must be attempted, and every description is an interpretation.

In his writings Niebuhr more than once undertakes an interpretation of Jesus Christ, but his finest contribution is probably found in *Christ and Culture.* Here he attempted to present a moral rather than a metaphysical or a historical description of Christ. His approach was to examine some of the phenomena in which the essence of Christ appears, and, being a moralist, the phenomena he chose were the virtues of Christ, by which he meant those excellences of character which Christ exemplified in his own life and which he communicates to his followers. He chose five virtues, each of which has been onesidedly emphasized by certain "schools" of theology. These were love (liberalism), hope (eschatological interpretations), obedience (existentialism), faith (orthodox Protestantism), and humility (monasticism). Taking each in turn Niebuhr showed how these virtues exemplified by Jesus Christ attained a radical meaning just because of his relation as Son to God the Father.

The penchant of liberal theology for describing Jesus wholly in terms of love stems from its tendency to identify God with love as a kind of all-inclusive fatherly goodwill, but Niebuhr denies that this "love of love" represents the theology of Jesus, for whom God is love but love is not God. Jesus' complete devotion is not to cosmic love, but to

God the Father, who alone is good but whose transcendent power would seem to those of lesser faith as anything but fatherlike. To love the One without whose will he would not have been crucified—this for Niebuhr indicates the greatness and the strangeness of Jesus' love of God! Of course, the virtue of love in Jesus' character and demand is not only seen in his love of God but also in his love of the neighbor in God. However, Niebuhr is quick to point out that in his teaching of the double commandment Jesus does not place these two loves on the same level. "It is only God who is to be loved with heart, soul, mind and strength," he said; "the neighbor is put on the same level of value that the self occupies" (CC, 17). Moreover, Jesus' love of man is not based on an imagined intrinsic value of the human soul but on the worth of man in relation to God. Thus Niebuhr thinks the Fourth Gospel was correct in changing the command from "Love thy neighbor as thyself" to "Love one another as I have loved you." More and more, Jesus' disciples came to see Jesus' love of man as God's own love of man. What we have are really two loves or two virtues with a common source:

> Love of God is adoration of the only true good; it is gratitude to the bestower of all gifts; it is joy in Holiness; it is "consent to Being." But the love of man is pitiful rather than adoring; it is giving and forgiving rather than grateful; it suffers for and in their viciousness and profaneness; it does not consent to accept them as they are, but calls them to repentance. The love of God is nonpossessive *Eros;* the love of man pure *Agape;* the love of God is passion; the love of man, compassion. There is duality here, but not of like-minded interest in two great values, God and man. It is rather the duality of the Son of Man and Son of God, who loves God as man should love Him, and loves man as only God can love, with powerful pity for those who are foundering (CC, 18f.).

The second virtue that Niebuhr discussed was that of hope. Eschatologists such as Albert Schweitzer have depicted Jesus in terms of intense expectancy rather than love. They believe that Jesus' preaching and ethical teachings were animated by his great hope that God would soon fulfill his Messianic promise by establishing his kingdom on earth. Niebuhr agreed that Jesus Christ as described in the New Testament was a man of hope, but he disagreed with the eschatologists' view that his hope was founded on a dogmatic conception of history which stressed the shortness of time before the supernatural consummation of the kingdom. Jesus' hope was based not on a view of history but on God himself, who would reveal his righteousness and manifest his divine glory. Indeed, said Niebuhr, much of Jesus' hope had to do not with the coming kingdom but with the present rule of God in everyday natural events. The important thing was his relation to the God who is Now as well as Then, present as well as future. "Not eschatology but sonship to God is the key to Jesus' ethics," declared Niebuhr (CC, 22).

Just as Niebuhr recognized the evident truth of ascribing the virtues of love and hope to Jesus, so he acknowledged the truth of the Christian existentialists' claim that Jesus was a man of radical obedience. His was an obedience even unto death, for he had come not to do his own will but the will of his Father. Nevertheless, Niebuhr objected to the tendency of existentialists like Rudolf Bultmann to concentrate on the virtue of obedience to the exclusion of other virtues and to empty the will of God of any content. The existentialist Jesus is more Kantian than the Jesus of the Gospels. To be sure, it is God who is to be obeyed, but in this view God becomes the mere counterpart of moral decision, the "Unconditioned" or the Power who constrains decision. That is, the idea of God is as formal and empty as the idea of obedience. To turn Jesus into an existentialist with this twentieth—century ethics of freedom is, in Niebuhr's judgment, nothing less than a caricature of the New Testament Christ, who knows a great deal about the character and the will of the God to whom he is radically obedient. God's will is that of the Creator and Governor of all nature and all history; it has structure and content. Moreover, God is the author of the Ten Commandments; he demands mercy and not sacrifice; and he requires not only obedience but love and faith. In short, Jesus' obedience is that of a Son whose sonship is not definable in terms of a principle that constrains obedience but of a Father who bestows the gifts that make obedience possible.

When Niebuhr turns to the Protestant emphasis on the faith of Jesus Christ and the monastic interest in his great humility, he also finds that Jesus' faith and humility are inordinate precisely because of his relationship to God. The New Testament indicates that Jesus had little faith in the goodness of men but was heroic in his faith in God, whom he called Father. Free of anxiety, he relied on God for his daily needs and trusted him to the end, finally commending his spirit to him who he knew was responsible for his shameful death. This extreme faith was matched by a radical humility. Niebuhr pointed to his living with sinners and pariahs, his washing of the disciples' feet, and his acceptance of indignities from the priests and soldiers. Yet the humility of Jesus is a humility before God, the humility of a Son. In his conduct of life, stressed Niebuhr, there was not the slightest sign of a feeling of inferiority before men, no lack of confidence, servile condescension, or defensiveness. "The humility of Christ," wrote Niebuhr, "is not the moderation of keeping one's exact place in the scale of being, but rather that of absolute dependence on God and absolute trust in Him, with the consequent ability to remove mountains. The secret of the meekness and the gentleness of Christ lies in his relation to God" (CC, 27).

Although any one of these five virtues can be taken as the key to understanding Christ's character and teaching, Niebuhr advocated taking them together and recognizing that they all receive their significance from Christ's unique devotion to God. No figure of speech better symbolizes the reality of this unusual relationship than "Son of God," and Niebuhr pointed out that in his sonship Jesus Christ is mediatorial. That is, as a single person he is the "focusing point" in a continuous alternation of two movements: one from men toward God and the other from God toward men. On the one hand, to know Jesus Christ as the Son of God is to be directed toward the Father; on the other, because he is the moral Son of God in his love, hope, faith, obedience, and humility in the presence of the Father, he is the moral mediator of God's will toward men. Niebuhr described Jesus' moral mediatorship in this beautiful passage:

> Because he loves the Father with the perfection of human *eros,* therefore he loves men with the perfection of divine *agape,* since God is *agape.* Because he is obedient to the Father's will, therefore he exercises authority over men, commanding obedience not to his own will but to God's. Because he hopes in God, therefore he gives promises to men. Because he trusts perfectly in God who is faithful, therefore he is trustworthy in his own faithfulness towards men. Because he exalts God with perfect human humility, therefore he humbles men by giving them good gifts beyond all their deserts. (CC, 28).

Niebuhr was convinced that an adequate description of Jesus Christ would necessitate other approaches than the moral one but that, regardless of the approach, the same issue would come to the fore, namely, the issue of his sonship and his mediatorship. Jesus Christ's power and attraction does not come from him alone, but from him as the Son of the Father; he is at once man living to God and God living with men. Niebuhr's conception of Christ as the moral Son of God, which is set forth most broadly in *Christ and Culture,* is also found in other major works. In *Radical Monotheism and Western Culture* he described Christ as the incarnation of radical faith, and in *The Responsible Self* Christ is pictured as the responsible man *par excellence.* Both of these deserve closer scrutiny.

Incarnation is defined by Niebuhr as "the coming of radically monotheistic faith into our history, meaning by it the concrete expression in a total human life of radical trust in the One and of universal loyalty to the realm of being" (RMWC, 40). Radical faith, according to him, was incarnate to a limited extent in the life of Israel, since for this people all human relations were transformed into convenantal relations which involved the giving and the keeping of promises. Religion itself was understood in terms of a covenant between God and the people. In Jesus Christ, however, radical faith was incarnate to a far greater extent, because in him the word of God as God's oath of fidelity became flesh. By this Niebuhr meant that Jesus was a man "who single-mindedly accepted the assurance that the Lord of heaven and earth was wholly faithful to him and to all creatures, and who in response gave wholehearted loyalty to the realm of being" (RMWC, 42). It was Niebuhr's conviction that such confidence and loyalty can only be that of a son of God.

In his Earl Lectures, portions of which are appended to *The Responsible Self,* Niebuhr related the meaning of Jesus Christ to the symbol of responsibility. He noted that when Christ is viewed from this perspective, he is again involved in the double movement from man to God and from God to man. Jesus is the responsible man who in all his responses to alteractions did what fitted into the divine action; yet he interpreted every alteration that he encountered as a sign of the action of God, that universal, omnificient One whom he called Father. Thus Jesus Christ is, as the editor of these Lectures suggests, the "paradigm of responsibility" (RS, 162). He exemplifies an ethics of responsibility to the living God who is present in all the many actions upon man. However, Niebuhr pointed out that Christ is more than the responsible man for Christians. They believe that he performs that strange miracle of reconciling them to God, of changing their deep distrust and disloyalty into faith in the Determiner of destiny. Through Christ's life, death, and resurrection, men come to know God as their Father and thus to know themselves as sons of God who are heirs in the universe and at home in the world. An at-one-ment occurs. Men are released from their bondage to the false gods and are brought into a right relationship with their Creator.

Precisely how Jesus Christ accomplishes the reconciliation of men to God and of God to men was not clear to Niebuhr, and he found none of the church's traditional theories of the atonement wholly satisfactory. He abhorred those theories that picture God as a destructive and angry potentate whose ordering of the universe is one of retribution in which goodness is rewarded and evil punished. No, the God of Jesus is the forgiving Father of prodigal children whose order is one of graciousness whereby the sun is made to shine on evil and on good and the rain to descend on the just and the unjust alike.

The cross is usually at the center of any theory of atonement, and it is only natural to ask about Niebuhr's understanding of the cross of Christ. Although he recognized that its meaning involved more than this, he at least affirmed that the cross raised with extreme intensity the questions of whether God is good and whether goodness is powerful. "To some of us," he wrote, "it seems that in the cross of Jesus Christ, in the death of such a man who trusts God and is responsible to him as a son, we face the great negative instance or the negation of the premise that God is love, and that unless this great negative instance— summarizing and symbolizing all the negative instances—is faced, faith in the universal power of God must rest on quicksand; in facing it, however, we have the demonstration in this very instance of a life-power that is not conquered, not destroyed" (RS, 176f.). God the Father of Jesus Christ manifests his ultimate power by resurrecting his son from the dead. Niebuhr stressed, however, that the resurrection is not manifest to us in physical signs but in Jesus Christ's continuing Lordship. Through him men are empowered to become sons of God. Sins are forgiven, and friendship is established between God and man and between man and man. God the enemy becomes trusted as God the friend.

Niebuhr emphasized that reconciliation to God is reconciliation to life itself, that love of God is "love of being, rejoicing in existence, in its source, totality and particularity . . . conviction that there is faithfulness at the heart of things: unity, reason, form and meaning in the plurality of being" (PCM, 37). Faith in God involves one's whole life in a continuous revolution. Remorse becomes repentance, self—love turns into love of God and love of neighbor, fear of death is replaced by the assurance of eternal life. Taboos are removed from intellectual life, so that all knowledge becomes reverent and all being open to inquiry. The values which polytheism made absolute are relativized, so that the strife of the gods comes to an end. At the same time, however, a new sacredness attaches to the relative goods, for whatever is, is now known to be good. "The moral consequences of faith in God," declared Niebuhr, "is the universal love of all being in him" (RMWC, 126).

The revolution and conversion of life brought about by the Christian revelation also involves the overcoming of the evil imaginations of the heart by the new image of God in Christ which enables the heart to understand. In an unusually beautiful and striking passage in *The Meaning of Revelation* (pp. 109-132) Niebuhr explained how revelation brings a pattern of dramatic unity to the history of the self. "Whatever else revelation means," said Niebuhr, "it does mean an event in our history which brings rationality and wholeness into the confused joys and sorrows of personal existence and allows us to discern order in the brawl of communal histories" (MR, 109). First, our past becomes intelligible. Not only does revelation unify and make understandable all we can remember from our past life, but it also forces us to recall the unpleasant events we had forgotten or repressed and to bring them within the scope of our understanding. Furthermore, through Jesus Christ we are able to accept the entire human history as our own, appropriating the past of all human groups, whether Hebrews or Greeks, slaves or free, Europeans or

Africans, medieval or modern men. Nothing is alien to us.

Niebuhr pointed out that the work of apprehending and interpreting the past in terms of the revelatory moment is not merely an intellectual exercise, but a moral event in which the soul is reconstructed. The past we remember through Jesus Christ is not the serial but the enduring past, that is, the past that is what we are, our constitution and inheritance. Conversion of the past, said Niebuhr, is not something that is completed once and for all, but something in which the reasoning heart must continually be engaged. Why? Because the past is infinite, but also because sin enters into history ever anew as we separate ourselves from God and our neighbors by separating our past from them. Niebuhr was convinced that the hope for church reunion, and, beyond that, the reunion of the human race, lies in the corporate remembering of our entire past, with all its sins, through Jesus Christ and the subsequent acceptance and appropriation of each others' pasts.

The revelatory moment also makes our present intelligible. Our evil imagination not only hides from us what we are, i.e., our past, but also what we are presently doing and suffering. Niebuhr poignantly pointed out that the words of Jesus on the cross, "Father, forgive them, for they know not what they do," are applicable to us in every moment. We never know fully the consequences of our actions and our inactions, and we tend to justify what we do and fail to do in terms of a picture we ourselves have drawn. A true assessment of the present is possible only when the self is removed from the center of things and our actions are seen in the light of the larger image given in revelation. The life and death of Christ becomes a parable or analogy by which we can interpret our own present.

Beyond bringing intelligibility into our past and present, revelation also makes possible an interpretation of the future. Niebuhr knew full well, of course, that the future we see is not ours directly but is the future of him who has revealed himself to be the Lord of life and death. However, in his overcoming of death Jesus Christ invests our own history with a hope that is inextinguishable, for in him we glimpse the resurrection of a new and other self, of a new community, a newborn remnant.

Christ and Culture

The grace of God revealed in Jesus Christ was considered by Niebuhr to be not only the converter of man's understanding of his personal and communal history but also the converter of man's culture. This conclusion can be drawn from Niebuhr's book, *Christ and Culture,* in which he distinguished five prominent attitudes that Christians have assumed toward culture, which he defined broadly as that total process and total result of human activity that comprises "language, habits, ideas, beliefs, customs, social organization, inherited artifacts, technical processes, and values" (CC, 32). Culture is what the New Testament often calls "the world," that social heritage which assumes many forms and to which all men are inevitably subject. In order to understand Niebuhr's position more adequately, it will be helpful to elucidate his five types of relationships between Christ and culture.

At one end of the attitudinal spectrum Niebuhr places radical Christianity, which sets Christ against culture and advocates Christian withdrawal from any contact with the sinful world and its cultural tasks. This view is found in primitive Christianity, which separated itself from Roman society, and runs through the monastic and sectarian movements to the modern rejection of culture by Tolstoy. At the opposite end of the spectrum Niebuhr puts cultural Christianity, which portrays a Christ of culture and seeks an accommodation with the prevailing culture without sanctioning the whole. As representatives of this view Niebuhr named the early Christian Gnostics, the medieval theologian Abelard, Albrecht Ritschl's "cultural Protestantism," and those American Christians who tend to identify the American and the Christian ways of life. The Christ of culture is looked upon as the great moral teacher and leader of cultural causes rather than the radical who calls Christians to separate themselves from the world and its hopelessly wicked ways.

Between the two extremes of radical separation and cultural accommodation Niebuhr proposed three mediating positions which represent the majority of Christians. This majority group holds a number of convictions in common. First, they believe that the paramount issue concerns the relation between God and man rather than between Christ and culture. They argue that if the Father of Jesus Christ is the Creator of the world, then the world of nature and culture cannot be all bad. On the contrary, it is just in their natural, cultural lives that men are called to be obedient to God. Second, these Christians of the center agree that sin is both universal and radical. For any group of human beings to think they can seal themselves off from sin by withdrawing into a holy ghetto or to assume that sin does not penetrate to the depths of human personality is a manifestation of gross naiveté as well as folly. Finally, these Christians affirm both the primacy of God's grace and the necessity of man's works of obedience in the cultural sphere. They cannot separate God's grace from man's cultural activity, nor man's cultural activity from God's grace. Differences appear, however, in the analyses of how these are related.

The three mediating positions set forth by Niebuhr were the following: the synthetist, the dualistic, and the conversionist. The synthetist affirms both Christ and culture but makes it clear that Christ is above culture. The relation is hierarchical yet harmonious, so that the Christian's belief in God-in-Christ and his concern for the affairs of the world can proceed apace. His exalted view of Christ separates him from cultural Christianity, and his appreciation of culture distinguishes him from radical Christianity. Niebuhr mentioned Clement of Alexandria and Thomas Aquinas as the outstanding theologians of synthetic Christianity, which has been the dominant position in Roman Catholicism and in much of Anglicanism.

Dualistic Christianity, according to Niebuhr, holds Christ and culture in a paradoxical relationship. For the dualist the basic issue of life is not the relation of the Christian to culture but the relation between God and man, or, better, between God and us. He begins with the miracle of God's grace, the great act of reconciliation and forgiveness wrought in and through Jesus Christ; but he believes that despite the revelation of God's grace and the new beginning it brings, the grace remains God's and the believer continues to be subject to sinful corruption. To speak paradoxically, the Christian is, at one and the same time, a justified man and a sinner. Like the radical Christian the dualist pronounces the whole world of culture to be godless and sick unto death, but unlike the radical he knows that he belongs to culture and that the gracious God sustains him in it and by it. As prominent representatives of this position Niebuhr named Paul the Apostle, Martin Luther, Søren Kierkegaard, and Ernst Troeltsch. In his opinion the greatest is Luther, a dynamic, dialectical thinker who distinguished but did not divide life in Christ and life in culture, the kingdom of God and the kingdom of the world. Niebuhr emphasized that in Luther's thought, unlike that of some of his followers, the spiritual and the temporal realms are continually interacting with one another.

Niebuhr's third mediating type is conversionist Christianity, which believes that Christ transforms culture. It is this positive and hopeful attitude toward culture that distinguishes the conversionist from the dualist, and Niebuhr was convinced that this attitude was closely connected with certain theological views about creation, the fall of man, and history. For the conversionist, God's creative and ordering activity is as major a theme as his atoning work, whereas the dualist tends to place so much emphasis on atonement that creation becomes a mere prologue to it. The dualist also brings creation and fall into such close proximity that he is tempted to speak as if the creation of the finite world involved a fall away from God, whereas the conversionist makes a sharp distinction between creation and fall. For him the fall is entirely the action and responsibility of man, and the result of the fall is a corruption and perversion of what is good. The conversionist looks upon man's culture as corrupted order; the dualist often seems to view it as order for corruption. Finally, history for the conversionist is not a course of merely human events but the story of God's mighty deeds and of man's response to them. If the dualist thinks of history primarily as the time of struggle between faith and unfaith, of life between promise and fulfillment, the conversionist sees it as a time of dramatic interaction between God and man and believes that in history all things are possible to God. The dualist lives more "between the times," the conversionist more in the divine Now, aware that the Lord has the power to transform all things, including human culture, by lifting them up to himself.

It would seem that Niebuhr was least attracted to radical Christianity and successively more attracted to cultural, synthetic, dualistic, and conversionist Christianity. He admired the radicals for maintaining the crucial distinction between Christ and Caesar, but he could not accept their withdrawal from the world and its cultural tasks. Cultural Christians seemed to him to provide an important witness to the "cultured among the despisers of religion" and to make known the universal meaning of the gospel, but he could condone neither their watered-down views of Jesus and of sin nor their tendency to portray the basic human problem as a conflict between spiritual forces and nature.

More congenial to Niebuhr than either of these extremes were the three positions in the center. The over-all balance achieved in the synthetist's position was attractive to him:

the synthesis of reason and revelation, the harmony between one's view of the world and his belief in God, the continuity between nature and supernature, the intelligible basis for cooperative work with nonbelievers. Nevertheless, he also found in this position some serious weaknesses. His major objection was that in the synthetist's effort to bring Christ and culture into one system of thought and action he tended to absolutize what is relative, to reduce the infinite to finite form, to materialize what is dynamic. The temporal and human tends to usurp the place and power of the eternal and divine, and the problem of the presence of radical evil in everything human is not faced. Moreover, Niebuhr detected in the synthetist position a tendency toward cultural conservatism, stemming quite naturally from tendencies to equate a cultural view of God's law with that law itself and to be more concerned with the defense of the culture synthesized with the gospel than with the gospel itself. For Niebuhr these inherent dangers outweighed the appealing features of the synthetist position, which seemed in the end to lead to the institution-alization of Christ and the gospel.

To say whether a true son of the Reformation is more a dualist or a conversionist is not always an easy matter. The two types hold so much in common and their differences are so subtle that it is not impossible for the same man to appear to represent each at different times under differing circumstances during his life. To attempt to say which is "better" is like trying to decide between Paul and John or Luther and Calvin—or between Reinhold and H. Richard Niebuhr! In his exposition of the dualistic position Niebuhr was appreciative of its virtues. He pointed to its dynamic understanding of the relation between God and man and between sin and grace, its focus on the profundity and power of the work of Christ as well as on the depth and viciousness of human depravity, its setting forth of an ethics of action, and its periodic reinvigoration of both Christianity and culture. All in all, Niebuhr believed that its depiction of the dilemmas and tensions of human life "before God" corresponded closely to experience.

On the other hand, Niebuhr perceived in dualism the dangerous tendency to lead Christians into antinomianism and into cultural conservatism. If Christians consider all laws of society and of reason and all human works to be relativized by the doctrine that, before God, everything human is sinful, then they are tempted to disregard laws altogether and thus to cast aside the rules of civilized living. Another alternative, equally unsatisfactory, is to look upon the law, the state, and other institutions as mere restraining forces against sin rather than as agents of positive social reform through which the neighbor can be helped toward true life. The realm of Christ and the realm of Caesar can be so separated through dualistic thinking that Christians of this persuasion feel little civic responsibility. Finally, Niebuhr reiterated his belief that the dualist tends to move creation and fall so close together that everything temporal and finite is thought to be sinful, with the result that justice is not done to the ever-present creative and sustaining activity of God.

There can be no doubt that the understanding of Christ and culture expressed in the conversionist type of Christianity is closer to Niebuhr's own theology than any other. Here Christ is not only the redeemer of man from the bondage of sin and death, but also the great transformer of human life, the regenerator and sanctifier of man in his culture. This is the view found in much of Augustine's work, in John Calvin and John Wesley, in Jonathan Edwards and Frederick Denison Maurice, and it was in the company of these Christian scholars and churchmen that Niebuhr felt most at home.

Like the conversionist, Niebuhr believed that every man, whether he acknowledges it or not, lives under the creative power and sovereign rule of God-in-Christ and Christ-in-God. Like the conversionist, he believed that man is created good and that through his own act of sinful defection from God his good nature and his culture become twisted, warped, perverted, and corrupted. The problem of man and his culture is not solved by destruction and new creation, but by transformation and redirection. Finally, like the conversionist, Niebuhr believed that this conversion is possible in history. The ongoing interaction between God and man provides the basis for transformation, and for Niebuhr it is the church that is called to lead the way by living a transformed life.

The Church

As a result of God's action in and through Jesus Christ, the church comes into being. Much of Niebuhr's writing is devoted to questions concerning the church, and he is often as emphatic about what the church is not as he is about what it is. First, the church is not the kingdom of God. "The Church is no more the kingdom of God," declared Niebuhr, "than natural science is nature or written history the course of human events" (PCM, 19). God's kingdom is his sovereign rule which, although hidden, is still the reality behind and in all realities. It is the rule of the Creator and the Redeemer, of the One who has the power over life and death, and it is the rule that is over-all and eternal. In no sense does the church share in this reign. Instead, the church is in Niebuhr's view that part of the human race that believes that the hidden kingdom was revealed in convincing fashion in Jesus Christ, that attempts to live according to the will of God in the present, and that looks forward to the coming of the kingdom in power. The church is, in Niebuhr's words, "the subjective pole of the objective rule of God" (PCM, 19). That is, the church is the subject that apprehends, worships, sometimes imitates, and sometimes reflects its Object, but it also sharply distinguishes itself from this Object.

Second, the church is not the only human community

that is directed toward the divine reality. Niebuhr abhorred any attitude of triumphalism, exclusivism, or superiority on the part of Christians. For him the uniqueness of the church lies in its particular relationship to the divine reality, namely, the relationship which is inseparable from Jesus Christ. The church is that particular human community that has Jesus Christ as its center and whose knowledge of God comes through him. This is a special knowledge that is unknown from other perspectives: knowledge of "the reconciling nature and activity of a God who is Father and Son, and also Holy Spirit" (PCM, 20). Niebuhr was convinced that just this Trinitarian understanding of the divine reality makes evident how inadequate and misleading it is to define God in terms of Jesus Christ alone.

In an article called "The Norm of the Church" (1946–1947), Niebuhr provocatively declared that the church is not primarily a religious community whose religion centers in Jesus Christ, but it is simply a community that centers in him. In his opinion the church is better described as a moral instead of a religious community, because its relation to Jesus Christ is primarily not one of worshiping him but one of embodying his mind and spirit, his faith and hope and desire. Thus any human association becomes church when Jesus Christ is its center. This means that whenever family groups, workers' associations, schools, or any other community begin to ask what Jesus Christ requires of them, they have become church, regardless of whether they are in close touch with some religious institution. For Niebuhr the central presence of Jesus is the norm of the church, but he was convinced that throughout the centuries undue attention had been paid to religious practices as mediators of this presence. He expressed his own view in this passage:

> Acts of charity, the giving of cups of cold water (by those who can afford no milk or wine), the healing of diseases, and above all acts of forgiveness of the enemy and the seeking and saving of the

lost must rank as high as notes of the presence of the church as the traditional marks of correct rites and right order.[11]

From this it should come as no surprise that Niebuhr did not identify the church *tout court* with the churches. However, he affirmed a close interrelationship and confessed that though the claim of the churches to be the sole representatives of the church on earth must be denied, he knew of no way to aspire after membership in the church without joining one of the churches. In his first book, *The Social Sources of Denominationalism,* Niebuhr convincingly documented the fact that the denominations that we call churches are less the products of the mind and spirit of Jesus Christ that those of various social, political, economic, and racial factors. He branded the divisiveness represented by denominationalism a moral failure on the part of Christians. Despite this failure, however, Niebuhr still knew that he could not speak of the church apart from the churches, and in an article entitled "The Hidden Church and the Churches in Sight" (1945–1946) he attempted to elucidate the paradoxical relationship between them.

Niebuhr began by indicating some understandings of the relationship which he considered erroneous or inadequate. The first is to identify one's own religious organization with the true church while ascribing all the contradictory features to other religious groups. Another is to assign the being of the church to the realm of ideality while regarding the churches as belonging to the realm of sense experience. A third, which has been popular in Protestantism, is to differentiate between a visible and an invisible church, that is, between the human institution and the church of faith. Although Niebuhr had some sympathy with this view, he felt that the relation between the two churches had never been adequately worked out. In part the distinction seemed to be between the church known only to God and the church which is known to men as full of hypocrites and not true, in part between the work of God and the work of men, that is, between the community that God has chosen and the institution created by the preachers and the elders.

In developing his own doctrine of the church, Niebuhr attempted to recognize the validity of distinguishing between the visible churches and the invisible church while at the same time offering an interpretation that was more adequately grounded in recent biblical studies and studies in the sociology of religion. He believed that two ideas were essential to any satisfactory theory of the Church. The first is that the church is an eschatological society or, better, an emergent reality, hidden yet real. Just as Jesus as the Christ is the ever-present one who has come and yet is still to come in glory, and just as the Christian life is "hid with Christ in God" and yet is something to be counted on, so the church is a reality which is not yet at hand but is at the very edge of coming into existence, more real than all the communities that are passing away. It is the society of the new order of creation in which all things shall become and are new, and even though we do not yet see it, we can count on it because in a sense it is the only world that is real.

The second idea considered essential by Niebuhr is that the religious institutions called the churches are subject to a constant process of conversion, that is, a turning of the mind and heart toward God-in-Christ, toward faith and obedience. The churches, explained Niebuhr, are not the converted parts of society, but the parts in which conversion makes its appearance in religious form. This conversion is not an isolated event but a process that accompanies the whole of Christian life as it stands under the continuing impact of the gospel of the kingdom of God. Niebuhr clarified what he meant in these words:

> Our Christian churches, so-called, are like ourselves, just human entities on which God has taken mercy and which he is converting to himself. In them and through them we sin and falter as we do in and through our families and our states. But in and through them we can serve the Church of our faith as we can nowhere

else. The preaching of the gospel, the administration of the sacraments, and the provision of a decent order—these are not the signs of the presence of the great Mother of us all, the Church of God, but they are the duties we can perform in order to minister to that Church and to declare our faith in its presence.[12]

In the light of his understanding of the interrelation of the church and the churches, Niebuhr concluded that Christians should be characterized by a double attitude: sorrow and repentance in and for the churches, but confidence and joy in the church.

The church has traditionally been said to be one, holy, catholic, and apostolic. When arguing that the church is not an ideal but, rather, an object of faith and love and an anchor of hope, Niebuhr presented his own interpretation of these traditional "marks" of the church, although he substituted "Christian" for "apostolic." The oneness of the church means that "it unites us with all our fellow men and that it unites all men in loyalty to one God. It is one in the sense that it brings us into harmony and unity with the Creator and with Christ and with the Holy Spirit and that all these are present in it." Its catholicity means that "nowhere upon earth and at no time shall we or our children or our neighbors be left without ministers of the grace of Christ and without witnesses to faith." The holiness of the church means that it is "the holy company of those who receive a constant forgiveness and cleansing of their sins and who in measureless gratitude for measureless love forgive as they have been forgiven." Finally, to say that the church is Christian means that it is the community "of which Christ is the center, the brain, and the heart; he thinks in it and it feels as he does; his mind works in its searchings after truth and his self-forgetfulness inspires all its actions."[13] Niebuhr emphasized that this church is not an ideal but a reality we can count on. It is not something we can strive to bring into existence, for it is before us.

The research that Niebuhr and his colleagues conducted on Protestant theological education in the United States and

Canada revealed a bewildering variety of understandings of the purpose of the church. Some people defined its goal individualistically as the salvation of souls, others socially as the realization of the redeemed society. Some said its purpose was to build up the corporate life of the congregation, others to communicate the redeeming doctrines of the Bible. Some said its aim was to gain followers of Jesus Christ, others to proclaim Christ's Lordship. Although he recognized an element of truth in all these definitions, Niebuhr was satisfied with none. His own reflections on the question of the purpose of the church finally led him to a simple yet profound statement which he set forth in *The Purpose of the Church and Its Ministry*. The goal of the church, he declared, is "the increase among men of the love of God and neighbor" (PCM, 31).

Niebuhr's definition underscored some of his deepest convictions. In the first place, the church is to be identified not with a stable institutional organization once and for all established but with a dynamic movement Godward and in God's name worldward. Only such a movement can express faith in the sovereignty of God, who has loved us and who calls us to love in return. Moreover, to define the purpose of the church as the increase among men of the love of God and neighbor makes crystal clear the fundamental interrelatedness of self, neighbor, and God. It emphasizes Niebuhr's contention that for Christian thinking no member of this triad can be thought, known, or loved except in relation to the other two. Finally, implicit in this definition is the fact that love of God and neighbor is both law and gospel. That is, it is both the demand laid upon man by the sovereign God and the gift that God makes of himself through Jesus Christ. It is at once the good news of God's unfailing love for man and the requirement of a response of reciprocal love, however faltering and incomplete.

In explicating what his definition involved, Niebuhr described love as "rejoicing in the presence of the beloved, gratitude, reverence and loyalty toward him" (PCM, 35).

To love another is to rejoice over his very existence, to be thankful that he has given himself in companionship, to respect his otherness, and to be loyal to him and to his cause. To love God and neighbor is no easy matter, for we tend to love only the lovable and the loving. The problem of loving God is that we must love One on whom we are utterly dependent and yet who is the Mystery behind all the mystery of existence. How can one love God in the face of death, hardships of every kind, hostile neighbors, existence in a seemingly strange world the goodness of which appears questionable? This is possible, said Niebuhr, only if one is reconciled to God, which means that one is reconciled to life itself. If we love God, then we can love the neighbor. But who is the neighbor? Niebuhr tolerated no limitation on the definition of neighbor. The neighbor we should love is not only the near one but the far one, not just the friend but also the enemy, not only the familiar one but also the stranger. The neighbor is not only in the present but also in the past and in the future. He is not mankind in the abstract but in the particularity of individuals in community and of communities of individuals. Niebuhr even refused to limit the neighbor to men. The neighbor is all that participates in being, whether man or angel or animal or inorganic matter.

If the church is to achieve its grand purpose of increasing the love of God and neighbor among men, then it must not expend its efforts selfishly but must assume responsibility to God for the world. What this entails was never discussed more succinctly than in "The Responsibility of the Church for Society," an essay he contributed in 1946 to *The Gospel, the Church and the World,* a book edited by his Yale colleague, Professor Kenneth Scott Latourette. In dealing with the question of responsibility it is of course essential to know to whom one is responsible and for what one is responsible. In the case of the church the responsibility is to God, and it is this fact that sets the scope and defines the content of its responsiblity. Because the church is responsible to God-in-Christ, the scope of its responsibility is universal and infinite. No being existent in the world is outside its concern. But since the church is responsible to Christ-in-God, the content of its responsibility is always mercy. For Niebuhr this meant that the church is not responsible for the judgment or destruction of any beings in the world, but only for their conservation, reformation, redemption, and transfiguration.

In the light of this general description of the church's responsibility, how does Niebuhr depict its specific responsibility to society? There are two ways, he declared, that the church becomes socially irresponsible, namely, the way of worldliness and the way of isolationism. The worldly church substitutes human society itself for God-in-Christ, so that the "to whom" of responsibility is mistakenly defined. Instead of being responsible to God for society, it is responsible to society for God. In contrast, the isolated church seeks to respond to God solely for itself, regarding the secular societies around it as outside the divine concern. It was Niebuhr's belief that in the twentieth century, worldliness has been the greater threat to the church, since it has tended toward a conception of social responsibility that virtually made it an agent of secular culture. However, the remedy he advocated was not reformation by separation from the world, but a new entrance of the church into the world without conformity to it. The Church should be in the world but not of it. Its relation to God and to society should neither be confused nor separated, but is to be maintained in the unity of responsibility to God for the neighbor.

Niebuhr set forth his understanding of the church's responsibility for society in terms of its functions as apostle, pastor, and pioneer. In general terms its apostolic responsibility is to announce the gospel to all nations and to make them disciples of Christ. However, Niebuhr broke this down into more specific duties. First, the church is to proclaim as persuasively and imaginatively as possible that the center and heart of all things, the first and last Being, is utter goodness and complete love. Second, it is to convince mankind that the goodness that appeared in history in the form of Jesus Christ was not defeated but rose triumphantly from death. Third, it is to preach repentance, because Niebuhr was convinced that the good news about the glory of the divine goodness is neither rightly proclaimed nor rightly heard if it is not combined with the bad news about the great justice that prevails in God's world. Niebuhr stressed that the church's apostolic responsibility is not merely to individuals or to governments, but also to social groups such as nations and societies, although how to reach the latter is surely one of the church's most difficult problems.

The pastoral function of the church is discharged when, in Niebuhr's words, it "responds to Christ-in-God by being a shepherd of the sheep, a seeker of the lost, the friend of publicans and sinners, of the poor and broken-hearted."[14] Nevertheless, the church's pastoral interest does not stop with individuals. Indeed, just because of its responsibility to God for persons, it must be concerned for their social welfare, and this means becoming involved in political and economic issues and institutions. Moreover, Niebuhr pointed out that the church's responsibility for human societies is direct as well as indirect. For example, the church itself must initiate relief measures for needy nations and not simply call upon national governments to feed the hungry and to clothe the naked.

The third responsibility of the church is that of being a social pioneer, by which Niebuhr meant that the church is that part of the human community that responds first to God-in-Christ and Christ-in-God. Much as science is the pioneer in responding to pattern and rationality in experience and as artists are the pioneers in responding to beauty, so the church is the pioneer part of society that responds to God on behalf of the whole society. "It is that group," wrote Niebuhr, "which hears the Word of God, which sees His judgments, which has the vision of the resurrection."[15] Being the sensitive and responsive part in every society and in mankind as a whole, it assumes a representative role. On behalf of all men it moves toward God, worships, believes, and trusts God. It is the first to obey when it becomes aware of a new aspect of God's will and the first to repent for the sins of a society. Niebuhr believed that in all its representative and pioneering action the church is socially responsible when it functions as a world society, undivided by race, class, and national interests.

It seemed to Niebuhr that when the church truly functioned as pioneer, it assumed its highest form of social responsibility, since here it demonstrated the love of God and neighbor directly instead of repeating the commandment to itself and to others. Here the demonstration of faith is so concrete that there is no longer any question about the reality of the church. Here the invisible church becomes visible and the deed of Christ is reduplicated.

The Ministry

If the church is to fulfill its responsibility to God for society, if it is to carry out its apostolic, pastoral, and pioneering functions, if it is to attain its goal of increasing among men the love of God and neighbor, then the church must receive guidance. To be sure, ministering to the needs of the world on behalf of God is the task of all the Christians who make up all the congregations in all the churches on earth. In the deepest sense there is one ministry carried out by the one church whose Head is Jesus Christ, and this ministry is incumbent on every Christian by virtue of his membership in the universal priesthood of all believers. But in order for its ministry to be effective, the church has from the beginning found it necessary to set aside certain members to perform specific functions within and for the congregation. Thus there arose the office of the ordained minister, whose special ministry is intimately linked with and yet distinguished from the ministry of the laity.

The understanding of the role of the ordained minister has varied greatly throughout the history of the church, and in modern times the role has become problematic. Niebuhr attempted to deal creatively with this "perplexed profession" in *The Purpose of the Church and Its Ministry,* and this resulted in his offering a new image of the minister that would help bring about a fresh self-understanding concerning his role.

The dominant historical understanding of the minister which Niebuhr depicted in order to furnish a background for the modern crisis are those of pastoral ruler (or ruling pastor), priest, preacher of the Word, and evangelist. The idea of the pastoral ruler was formulated in *The Pastoral Rule* of Pope Gregory the Great (ca. 540-604) and provided the general concept of the minister for the medieval church. The pastoral ruler preached, administered the sacraments, taught, and led the worship service, but all of these activities were tailored to contribute to the chief ministerial function of the government of souls, the saving of souls from sin in this life and from hell in the next, which was best exercised through the penitential office. In contrast, the idea of the minister as priest, which became the controlling image in the Roman Catholic Church after the Reformation, presupposes the utter centrality of the work of administering the sacraments, particularly the offering of the sacrifice of Christ in the Eucharist. The priest also preaches, teaches, and governs souls, but everything he does is subordinate to his sacramental role of mediating the grace of God to man.

The churches of the Reformation were above all churches of the Word of God, and the minister of such a church, though performing most of the traditional functions, conceived his highest calling to be the preaching of God's good news to mankind, the gospel of the forgiveness of sin and of the reconciliation between man and God that was accomplished and revealed in and through Jesus Christ. Niebuhr conceded that preaching in the Reformation tradition was understood to include more than public discourse, but even so, this was the activity around which everything else was focused. Through the hearing of the Word of God's love for man came evangelical faith and renewal of life. The idea of the minister as evangelist, explained Niebuhr, developed in the Wesleyan, Evangelical, and Pietist movements and represents a variation on the Protestant conception of the preacher. The difference between them is mainly a matter of degree, the evangelist often traveling and confining his ministerial functions even more to preaching. His sermons were evangelical and intended to effect the conversion and sanctification of souls.

With this background in view Niebuhr moved to the problem of the ministry in the twentieth century. Whereas in the past the minister as pastoral ruler, priest, preacher, or evangelist had a clearcut idea of his most important function and of the proximate goal of all his activities, the modern minister has in many cases become uncertain about the nature and purpose of his ministry. Some blame his perplexity on the loss of Christian conviction or on anxiety over his professional status, others on the inroads of secular agencies into traditional ministerial functions or on the failure of the church to adjust to the needs of the modern world. While recognizing a measure of truth in each of these, Niebuhr insisted that the answer lay neither with those who would ignore cultural change nor with those who would abandon traditional functions. Rather, the real problem of ministers "is always how to remain faithful servants of the church in the midst of cultural change and yet to change culturally so as to be true to the Church's purpose in new situations" (PCM, 57).

Niebuhr was convinced that, despite the widespread

uncertainty about the ministry in the contemporary church, a new conception of the ministry was nevertheless gradually emerging. To what extent it was due, on the one hand, to cultural changes and, on the other, to new insights stemming from biblical and theological studies, he could not say, but the fact is that a view of the minister as "pastoral director" seemed to be taking hold in the churches, regardless of their denominational background. While holding no brief for the particular title, Niebuhr clearly felt that he could endorse the conception of the minister so designated and make it his own.

How are we to understand the idea of the minister as pastoral director? Niebuhr conjectured that perhaps no better clue to its meaning can be given than to contrast the architectural setting of the modern minister with that of his predecessors. Whereas the priest's place of ministry was a building or a room dominated by an altar and the preacher's a building or room dominated by a pulpit with its open Bible, today's minister works in a complex building which contains an office from which he directs the activities of the congregation and in which he studies and does some pastoral counseling. He of course still preaches, administers the sacraments, teaches, leads in worship, and presides over the church, but in all he does his main aim is to build up and direct a community toward the whole purpose of the church, namely, the increase among men of the love of God and neighbor. On the one hand, his interest is pastoral: to nourish, edify, build, and instruct his flock. On the other hand, his goal is to direct his flock in such a way that the total ministry of the church is carried out.

According to Niebuhr, the predecessor of the minister as pastoral director is to be found in the bishop or overseer of an ancient church, a man who was elected to oversee a single local congregation. The pastoral director is a minister of ministers, a teacher of teachers, a counselor of counselors, a servant of the servants of God. This conception makes it absolutely clear that the church itself is becoming and must become the minister in and to the world. Laymen, so-called, are the ministers who are most often in the best position to exercise responsibility to God for the world and to increase the love of God and neighbor. What laymen need is instruction, persuasion, counseling, and direction. To provide this is the task of the ordained minister.

How does the emerging conception of the minister as pastoral director differ specifically from earlier conceptions, particularly those of the preacher and priest? We have seen that he still carries out the traditional functions of the ministry but that he organizes them in relation to his central concern of building up or edifying the congregation. When Niebuhr examined the implications of this reorientation of ministry for the sake of our changed cultural situation, he first pointed to the difference that occurs in preaching. Preaching is no less important for the pastoral director, but it is now pastoral preaching. Its aim is not evangelical only, in the sense of being directed to sinners who need to be reconciled to God; it is this, said Niebuhr, but it is also calculated to help those who are becoming members of the body of Christ to become mature Christians who are able to interpret the Christian faith to others and generally to carry on the mission of the church in the world.

A second difference is that leading the church in worship becomes more important for the pastoral director than for the preacher. Rather than merely accompanying the preaching of the gospel, this worship is an effort of the church to demonstrate its love of God, and to do this effectively calls for creative leadership on the part of the minister. When it comes to his work with individuals, the pastoral director is, in Niebuhr's opinion, better designated a pastoral counselor than a pastoral ruler or a curer of souls. His concern is not merely with reconciliation to God but also with reconciliation to men, and in many cases guidance of the most varied kinds must be offered to people in need. Often his task is to refer his people to other agencies for help. As for his teaching responsibilities, the pastoral director is a teacher of teachers who cannot simply manage but must actually lead the educational organization of the church as a competent Christian educator.

Niebuhr also set forth the ramifications of the emerging conception of the ministry for the understanding of the minister's "call" and authority and for that of the church's tradition and people. The traditional interpretation, he explained, involves a fourfold call to the ministry: the general call to be a Christian, the secret call whereby a person is inwardly persuaded that God has summoned him to take up the work of the ministry, the providential call whereby the invitation to the ministry comes through the equipment of a person with the talents necessary for the exercise of the office and through the divine guidance of his life, and the ecclesiastical call, which is the summons given a person by the church to engage in its ministry. Niebuhr observed that in our day the ecclesiastical call, based on the church's understanding of a person's Christian and providential calls, was gaining in significance. Although the secret call remains important, it is the church, under the authority of God, that assumes the primary initiative in raising the question of the ministry with those young men and women whom God has endowed with the spiritual, moral, and intellectual qualities necessary for its work.

Sources of authority, declared Niebuhr, vary as widely as the different understandings of the ministry. In each instance there is one source that is primary, although it is usually combined with other sources that play a lesser role. The authority may be personal or ecclesiastical or scriptural, but these are all interrelated. For instance, the priest's authority is primarily institutional; it stems first from his church ordination, and only after that does one mention the personal authority of his life, his knowledge of

Scripture, or his understanding of the mind of the community. On the other hand, the pastoral ruler derived his authority primarily from his life of personal spiritual discipline, the preacher of the Reformation from his study and personal appropriation of Scripture, and the evangelist from his personal experience of the power of the gospel.

But what is the primary source of authority for the pastoral director? Niebuhr's answer is predictable. It is the community of the faithful that bestows authority on him. To be sure, although communal authority is of greatest importance to him, the pastoral director continues to be ordained by the institution, to be undergirded by an understanding of the mind of the church as expressed in Scripture and tradition, and to be strengthened by spiritual discipline. However, all of these are given special meaning because of the minister's relation to the community in which he does not rule but in which he is a director and a democratic pastoral administrator of a host of activities and leaders, all devoted to a common cause.

The final point raised by Niebuhr has to do with the people to whom ministers are sent. Who are they, and what is their greatest need? Is the minister sent primarily to the people of the church or to the world? Is the church inclusive, the servant of all, or exclusive, its ministry being confined to the elect? Here again Niebuhr reminded his readers of the various conceptions of man that have gone hand in hand with the different conceptions of the ministry. Gregory thought of man as an immature and sinful, though immortal, creature who needed a pastoral ruler to keep him on the course to heaven, whereas the Reformers considered man to be a sublime but perverted and rebellious creature whose basic need was to be reconciled to God through repentance and faith. In modern times, said Niebuhr, the tendency has been to think of man as primarily related to nature rather than to God, and even the churches and their ministers have often defined and attempted to meet the needs of man naturalistically and socially rather than theologically. But when man is defined on grounds other than the sovereignty of God or when one tries to make the gospel relevant to needs it never had primarily in view, then, in Niebuhr's judgment, confusion is inevitable.

What of the ministry today? To whom is the minister as pastoral director sent, and what is the paramount need of modern man? In view of Niebuhr's conception of the pastoral director given above, it is obvious that the people to whom he is sent are first the people of the church, but the church is conceived as a ministering community whose work is in the world. Thus the minister must always have his eye on both church and world, realizing that the relationship between the two is unique and ever changing. "What seems most evident in the case of the modern pastoral director," wrote Niebuhr, "is that he can think of himself neither as parish parson responsible for all the people in a geographic area nor as the abbot of a convent of the saved, but only as the responsible leader of a parish church; it is the Church, not he in the first place, that has a parish and responsibility for it" (PCM, 91).

Reflecting on man's nature and primary need in the mid-fifties, when he published *The Purpose of the Church and Its Ministry,* Niebuhr came to the conclusion that man was again coming to be understood as man-before-God. He wrote: "Out of the great wrestlings of men with their personal and social problems, out of renewed study of Scriptures and critical reflection on history, a view of man is emerging that sets in the forefront again his relation to God" (PCM, 78). This did not mean for Niebuhr the relinquishing of the important insights into human nature contributed by the natural and social sciences, but it meant a recognition that the depths of the mystery of man are not plumbed apart from his relation to the divine. With the emergence of this new, and yet old, understanding of man, the nature of the ministry also gains clarity, for men's needs become more definite. Niebuhr believed that there is a sense in which the fundamental needs of men, their aspiration after infinity and wholeness, do not change, although in another sense their needs do change in accordance with the changing forms in which they experience the ultimate dilemmas of their existence. The cry for salvation is the same, but it is phrased in many ways.

What is the form in which the cry is uttered and interpreted today? Niebuhr perceived several forms which expressed the needs of men to which the church must minister. The cry for salvation is the cry for life's meaning, for rebirth, for freedom from control by forces indifferent to their fate. It is the yearning to be free from bondage to all sorts of hidden forces and movements and powers that seem to direct the course of life and to determine its destiny, from the "other-directedness" and heteronomy of existence, from the life of mass man. All of these, said Niebuhr, indicate the ultimate human problems with which the ministry must grapple. These cries and yearnings help the church to understand its pastoral function, the language in which it must couch the gospel, and even the form it must assume in order to perform its service.

In 1960 Niebuhr had another opportunity to reflect on the world situation when he wrote his contribution to *The Christian Century's* series entitled "How My Mind Has Changed." On this occasion he emphasized the problem of men's deep disillusion about themselves and even about their idols, such as their nations and their scientific and technological prowess. Despite the multiplication of their powers over nature, men seemed no longer to expect these powers or the powers within themselves to save them from destruction or from the trivialization of existence. Niebuhr was convinced that more and more sensitive people were experiencing a great religious void, a feeling of extreme emptiness. In order for the church to meet the needs of the growing ranks of the disillusioned and the empty, Niebuhr was certain that the church must do more than simply become more orthodox or more liberal, more biblical or more liturgical. What was needed, he believed, was a resymbolization of the message and the life of faith in the one God. Retranslations of the old traditional terms would not suffice; somehow a resymbolization in pregnant words and in symbolic deeds must be achieved. Niebuhr confessed that he did not know how this would come about, but he did count on the Holy Spirit and did believe that the words and the deeds would be forthcoming. Furthermore, he was sure that without the revitalization of the human spirit from within, that is religiously, there could be no reformation of society.

Theology

If the church is to accomplish its mission, it must constantly be thinking about its message and its ministry. The reflection that goes on in the church Niebuhr calls "theology." Compared with other kinds of intellectual activity, theology is "the kind of thinking that is directed toward God and man-before-God as its objects and which is guided by the love of God and neighbor" (PCM, 109). Every Christian who thinks about his faith is *ipso facto* a theologian, and every Christian *must* think about his faith because reasoning is present in believing. But theology as a science is the special responsibility assumed by the leadership of the church, those pastoral directors who must preach and teach and counsel and generally guide the church in its ministry. To aid men and women in their preparation for leadership theological schools have long been established as centers for continuing study and practice.

For much of his life H. Richard Niebuhr was a practicing theologian in one of the great intellectual centers of America, and over the years he developed strong convictions about the nature and task of theology. In his judgment theology was nothing less than the exercise of the intellectual love of God and the neighbor, and he had little patience with a kind of anti-intellectualism in the church that would substitute piety for learning or social activity for hard thinking. Already in his contribution to *The Church Against the World,* which was published in 1935, he had this to say about the importance of theology:

> The revolters in the church are learning that without a Christian theory or theology the Christian movement must lose itself in emotions and sentiments or hasten to action which will be premature and futile because it is not based upon a clear analysis of the situation. They have learned from the communists that years spent in libraries and in study are not necessarily wasted years but that years of activity without knowledge are lost years indeed. They have learned from history that every true work of liberation and reformation was at the same time a work of theology (p. 153.)

Niebuhr was aware not only of the necessity of theology but also of its limitations. The reasoning of theologians, like any other reasoning, is historically conditioned. Theologians cannot think except as historic, communal beings subject to a given language and a given culture. They begin with revelation and faith, but the knowledge they receive is appropriated and understood within the framework of their own historicity, and there is no avoidance of their confessional stance or their limited point of view. Moreover, like the members of the church they serve, theologians are sinners to whom God has been merciful, and they can only hope to come to the truth by his grace. But though Niebuhr affirmed these limitations of theologians, he by no means regarded theology to be devoid of objectivity, a mere morass of subjective, relative judgment. On the contrary, theology was considered by him to be a science with its own peculiar objects, the intellectual pursuit of which was to be carried out with the highest possible degree of disinterestedness.

That the science of theology should be pursued disinterestedly was for Niebuhr a long-standing theme. However, for him disinterestedness did not mean uninterestedness. In an article called "Value-Theory and Theology" (1937) he declared that a theological science that is interested above all in serving the needs of men becomes a bad science incapable of supplying real benefits, whereas one that deals disinterestedly with its subject may be of great benefit. Disinterestedness is possible, he continued, only when the object excites interest for its own sake rather then for some end external to it. This same note is struck in *The Purpose of the Church and Its Ministry* when he speaks of theology as a "pure science." Like any other pure science, theology is disinterested in the sense that it concentrates on its objects for their own sake alone and seeks to exclude all extraneous, private interests. It is guided by the love of God and neighbor, not by self-love or the love of knowledge for its-own sake or the love of the neighbor-without-God. Indeed, Niebuhr insisted that it should not even be guided by the love of the church, but only by the church's love!

Niebuhr rejected the definition of Christian theology as the "science of God" on the grounds that it never has as its object God in isolation. Christians never know God-in-himself, God in his aseity, but only God in his relation to man. God alone is not the object of theology, but God and man—before—God. But even this is not an adequate specification for Niebuhr. The object of theology is complex and involves a triadic relationship: God in his relation to the self and the neighbor, and the self and the neighbor in relation to God; or even better: God in his relation to the self and its companions, and the self with its companions in relation to God. As has been pointed out previously, Niebuhr was convinced that theology cannot be reduced to Christology without grave distortion, though he did concede that the notion of Jesus Christ as "God-man" points symbolically to the complex object of theology.

Thus far only one of the functions of theology has been considered, namely, the exercise of the intellectual love of God and the neighbor which seeks to understand the faith of the church. According to Niebuhr there is a second indispensable function which operates in the realm of applied rather than pure science. This task of theology is to criticize faith in relation to its objects, which means to bring reflection and criticism to bear on other activities of the church, such as worship, preaching, teaching, and the care of souls. The church needs a theological understanding of each of these activities in order to see how they are interrelated within the total context of the ministry. This is especially essential for a pastoral director if he is to guide the various activities of the church toward a common goal. He must possess a unifying conception that is theologically grounded. The work of theology, however, does not stop with the positive elucidation of the church's practices. Niebuhr also stressed theology's critical and polemical role as a detector and corrector of perverted practices and of misunderstandings of church activities. Without constant surveillance and criticism the doings of the churches, like all human doings, fall victim to the sins of pride, sloth, and falsity. Nevertheless, this negative aspect of theology is rightly understood only when it is looked upon as ancillary to its positive task.

From Niebuhr's exposition of theology's double function it is obvious that he conceived of theology as the servant of the church. To serve the church by helping the church to serve God in the world is its primary responsibility, and most of Niebuhr's discussion of the nature and task of theology took place in the context of the education of ministers in theological schools. However, in an article that appeared in 1955 in the *Journal of Religion* he extended the discussion of theology beyond the confines of the church into the context of the university, and he did so with an appropriate title: "Theology—Not Queen but Servant'" The article was the manuscript of a convocation address delivered by Niebuhr in Rockefeller Chapel on the occasion of his receiving an honorary degree from the University of Chicago, and he was particularly concerned to interpret the place of the discipline of theology within a university. After disabusing his audience of the popular myth that during the Middle Ages theology reigned as queen over all other intellectual disciplines by pointing out that it was not theology but the empirical church that ruled the universities, Niebuhr discussed the place of theology within the modern university.

Niebuhr was convinced that a radically monotheistic theology offered human communities, whether they be intellectual, political, or religious, a way of understanding themselves that avoids the dangers of a complete pluralism or an absolute monism. This theology, which confesses the sole sovereignty of God and the ultimacy of God's Word, protests against the assumption of sovereignty by any finite power and against the presumption of any human voice to speak the ultimate word. Thus it opposes the imposition of any monistic overlordship. But at the same time theology opposes the ever-increasing fragmentation that results from what are essentially polytheistic allegiances to a pluralism of modern gods that go by the name of "values" or "powers." This theology does not stop with protest, however, but goes on to call attention to the way in which every individual, group, and institution is directly related, either positively in trust and loyalty or negatively in distrust and disloyalty, to God, whom Niebuhr here called the "Universal Sovereign" or the "Transcendent Universal." Acts of loyalty and confidence in the Transcendent, declared Niebuhr, are to be found in so-called secular activities as much as in religious ones, in citizens who place their highest loyalty in the universal commonwealth and in professors who count on the victory of universal truth and justice as much as in preachers and priests and theologians.

What would it mean for a university if it were controlled by a radically monotheistic faith? The result, claimed Niebuhr, would be a recognition by all sectors that they are related to one another in mutual service. A corollary to man's primary loyalty to the Universal and the

Transcendent is a loyalty to all being as emanating from one Source and proceeding to one End, and the consequence would be an equalitarianism in which each kind of being is entitled to reverence, understanding, and service, while it, in turn, is servant to the rest. However, in Niebuhr's view this would not exhaust the meaning of mutual service, because in such a university there would also be a common recognition that pretension to deity is universal among men and that therefore an acceptance of the duty to serve one another by mutual limitation and creative conflict is essential.

In the setting of this sort of university it is obvious that theology could not be a queen but only a servant. It would assume its place beside the other sciences and studies, not to be ministered unto but to minister. Theology, stressed Niebuhr, would know itself to be, first, a servant of God, but in its service to God it would also serve its fellow servants. It would be a servant of the church, helping the church to understand what it believes and maintaining a steady criticism of religion. But as a servant of the church under God, it is also the servant of the university and of the state, since not only the church is in the kingdom of God and since faith exists and does its work not only in the church. He elaborated what he meant in these words:

> Within the university, theology does not undertake to render service with the freedom of the uncommitted; but this is not a loss of freedom, since the wholly uncommitted are free only to serve themselves. It cannot seek truth for its own sake, but only for the sake of the divine glory—truth as reflection of the nature of being itself. In so far as it does that, seeking truth not for the sake of the church's glory or in order to glorify anything at all except the Transcendent Source and End of all things, its work in the university will not be less free than that of other inquiries. It ought to be the freest of all. As a fellow-servant of truth in this sense, theology takes its place in the university alongside other inquiries, never separated from them, never dependent upon them, never isolating itself with them from the totality of the common life which is the universe.[16]

Ethics

In the main H. Richard Niebuhr concentrated his teaching in the field of Christian ethics, but as an ethicist he was no less a theologian. For him theology and ethics were inseparable, even though they might be divided for the sake of instruction. The understanding of faith and the demands of love go hand in hand, just as love of God and love of neighbor may be distinguished but not separated. In Niebuhr's view Christian ethics directs its attention to the same complex object as theology: the interrelation of God, the self, and the neighbor. If, as he insisted, man is the creature who is responsible to God for his neighbor, then the framework for an ethics of responsibility is already given.

Before delving further into Niebuhr's ethics of responsibility, the best elaboration of which is found in the posthumously published book entitled *The Responsible Self,* it is important to note some of the characteristic emphases in his earlier ethical writings. In an article on "The Church in the World's Crisis" (1941) we find him advocating three general propositions regarding the duty of Christians in the face of political decisions. The first is that the religious issue at any particular time and place is less an issue about the specific content of actions than of the context in which each specific action is to be carried out. Actions, like words, derive their significance from the context in which they stand, and religious interest is directed more toward preceding and succeeding acts than toward the act of the moment. For example, in Jesus' story of the Pharisee and the publican *both* men pray, but the religious question concerns the total context in which they pray, that is, whether prayer is rendered in the context of trust in one's own goodness, being preceded by and directed toward other actions of self-aggrandizement, or in the context of faith in God's mercy. Or to take as another illustration the case of sex life, the religious question is not that of whether one should remain celibate or unite with another, but whether, regardless of the alternative chosen, the action taken is made part of a life of continuous responsibility so that it does not stand by itself but is made meaningful and effective in long devotion. Niebuhr's second proposition was that the important questions in the world crisis at that time, questions about the ownership of property and about war and peace, were religious questions in that they were questions about the context of political actions. By this Niebuhr meant that the great conflict was not between ideologies but between faiths, that is, between the religions of egoism, nationalism, and universalism. This leads to his final proposition, which was that the problem of Christians is to organize and shape their political actions in such a way that they will thereby express confidence in, and loyalty to, the Father of Jesus Christ as well as faith in the forgiveness of sins.

In 1950 Niebuhr published an essay called "Evangelical and Protestant Ethics," in which he contrasted a type of defensive "Protestant" ethics with a more positively oriented "evangelical" ethics. Since he obviously identified himself with the latter, the characteristics of evangelical ethics which he presented may be taken to represent his own convictions. He described evangelical ethics generally as "the mode of life which issues out of a positive relation to God, as that relation is established by, through, and with Jesus Christ."[17] He then proceeded to elaborate four specific characteristics. Evangelical ethics is, first, a *theocentric ethics,* that is, an ethics which accompanies a dominant orientation of the self and the community toward the action of God. Whereas some Christian ethical systems place the church or the Bible or religious experience or even sin at the center of attention, an evangelical ethics is strictly God-centered. Second, evangelical ethics is, according to Niebuhr, an *ethics of faith,* or, to be more specific, it is that mode of life that issues out of *faith in God.* To be sure, there are no faithless ethics, because all men live by some faith. However, everything depends on whether one's faith is in the transcendent God or in the false gods of the world. For this reason, insisted Niebuhr, evangelical ethics is not an ethics of faith per se, but, rather, an ethics of that faith in God which is given by, in, and through Jesus Christ.

Evangelical ethics is, third, an *ethics of freedom.* Freedom, wrote Niebuhr, is both a "freedom from" and a "freedom to." When faith in God is present, the self is free from concern for itself and is able to accept itself as a forgiven self. Along with freedom from self goes freedom from bondage to the physical and cultural values without which we think we cannot live. Our whole value system changes because it has a new center, namely, God, to whom we and the whole world are related. Finally, the self is freed from its bondage to the law. When man is directly related to God in faith, his whole understanding of the law is transformed. Niebuhr explained that prior to faith in God man is under the authority of moral traditions, of churches, and of states—the laws of men that make possible his survival mainly through prohibitions. But when man is bound to God and knows that God's law is the demand of One who is wholly good toward him, the spirit and the content of the law changes. Bondage turns into the freedom of sonship, and man's view of what is important and what is insignificant in life changes radically.

Niebuhr stated two things to which men are freed in the evangelical mode of life. First, they are freed to love their neighbor, and, second, they become free to deal creatively with the personal and social situations they encounter and to respond with inventiveness and artistry to the challenges they receive to meet the needs of their neighbor. "Creative morality," wrote Niebuhr, "is not bound by rule, though it knows all the rules. It does not meet the changing situations of life with the repetition of acts found good in the past, but with deeds that fit the immediate situation, recognized as a situation in the kingdom of God."[18]

The final characteristic of the evangelical mode of life is

what Niebuhr called its *momentariness*, by which he meant
that it is a life that does not plan far ahead to insure the
future, whether in heaven or on earth, but concentrates
instead on doing the right thing now. The neighbor is to be
loved here and now. The man who lives the evangelical life
knows that the future is in God's hands, that God ties the
present and future together because he is Lord of both, and
that the deed that seems temporally insignificant may have
more eternity in it than the one designed to outlast the
years. Over against what Niebuhr termed the world's melan-
choly wisdom that all our pomp is to be reduced to ashes,
evangelical ethics affirms "that what has been done to the
least of the brothers has been done unto him and that one
day in the Lord's sight may be a thousand years."[19] Niebuhr
fully recognized that such a life of momentariness would
appear reckless and offensive to our calculating human
reason, yet he declared it to be deeply wise in the context of
faith-knowledge.

Evangelical ethics, as the name implies, is an ethics deeply
informed by the gospel of Jesus Christ. It is above all an
ethics of freedom—that freedom for which Christ has set man
free. As a Christian, Niebuhr was thoroughly grounded in this
biblical understanding of ethics. But as a teacher of Christian
ethics he also knew that the subject could be approached
philosophically, and in the Introduction to *Christian Ethics,*
the sourcebook he co-edited and published in 1955, he distinguished two major types that have gained prominence in
the history of the church: the ethics of obligation and the
ethics of aspiration. The former is an ethics of "the right"
which asks about the requirement of the law or the lawgiver,
the latter an ethics of "the good" which asks about the end-
of-ends, the great and final goal. By the time he delivered the
Robertson Lectures in 1960, the manuscript of which was
later published as *The Responsible Self,* Niebuhr advocated a
third type of Christian ethics, viewed philosophically: the
ethics of responsibility. Throughout these lectures he contrasted three types of ethics and endeavored to demonstrate

the advantages of an ethics of responsibility over what he now called deontological ethics (the ethics of obligation) and teleological ethics (the ethics of aspiration).

If teleological ethics conceives man as an artificer or an artist who shapes his life according to an idea and for the sake of an end, and if deontological ethics views man as a citizen living under the law of his conscience which he must obey, then the ethics of responsibility thinks of man as one who is engaged in dialogue with another and who tries to make a proper response to the address of the other or to the other's action upon him. In the first type, man asks, "What is my goal, my ideal, my telos?" In the second, he asks, "What is the law and what is the first law of my life?" But in the third, he initially asks, "What is going on?" and then "What is the most fitting response I can make to what is happening?" Niebuhr pointed out that in the first type the tendency is to understand the self individualistically; in the second this is less the case, but man's relation to other selves is conceived as a relation under law; in the third the fundamentally social character of human existence is recognized, which means that the self is understood as existing primarily in relation to other selves.

Another important difference discussed by Niebuhr has to do with the relative importance of time and history in the three types of ethics. For teleological ethics, which emphasizes the realization of an ideal or goal, time is significant because man must reckon on the span of time available to him for the achievement of his inherent potentiality. Time and history assume less importance for deontological ethics, since man's duty to obey the law or to do the right is a rather formal demand, in which case time can be considered only a form of sense perception (Kant) or the meaning of all existence can be concentrated into the moment of decision (Kierkegaard). When man is defined primarily as a responder, as in the ethics of the fitting, the self is what Niebuhr calls "time-full." Here the past and the future are extensions of the present, that is, they are not the no-longer and the not-yet, but the still-present and the already-present. Time-full existence is an existence in encounter, so that to be in the present involves the compresence, through memory, of past encounters and the compresence, through anticipation, of future challenges and responses. Thus the self brings into the present its social past and is challenged to act in the future in a way that is fitting, but what the self considers fitting or unfitting response depends upon its understanding of its historical context. Changes in response patterns are possible, of course, only through reinterpretations of that context.

It is easy to understand why Niebuhr preferred as a prolegomenon for his Christian ethics the philosophical analysis of man as a responding, responsible being. Although part of his concern in *The Responsible Self* was to develop an instrument of analysis that would apply to any form of human life, he made clear from the beginning that he thought as a Christian and was interested in an analysis that would also aid in the understanding of the specifically Christian life. Without denying elements of truth found in the analysis of man as aspirer-after-a-goal or as man-under-law, or in the development of ethics in terms of "the good" or "the right," Niebuhr found the analysis of ethical man under the symbol of responsibility to be much more congenial to his theology. Here man is seen from the outset as essentially social, a being whose very selfhood is dependent on the action of an other upon him. He is challenged to respond, but the morality of that response depends on his interpretation of the action toward him, and, in turn, that interpretation depends on his understanding of the context in which he lives his life and within which the encounter takes place. The question of ethics is the question of the fitting response.

Transposed into a Christian key, Niebuhr can point to God's creation of man through his Word of love with the intent that man should respond in love both to his Creator and to his fellow creatures. His response is to be total trust in God and universal responsibility, discerning the action of

God in every action upon him and responding in a manner befitting this universal context. But man sins and falls away from God. His response becomes rebellious, distrustful, unconcerned, forgetful, and erratic; and his responsibility to God for others is abandoned in favor of selfish interests. As a self he lacks integrity, and his pattern of responses to others becomes fixed in accordance with his own narrowly conceived context. He is no longer free to change the pattern.

Yet God is not only the Creator but also the Redeemer. He reveals in and through his Son Jesus Christ not only his judgment upon sin but also his reconciling love for the sinner. Moreover, Jesus Christ brings to expression the true way of life for man. He is the responsible man *par excellence,* responding in love and trust to his Father and bringing the universal love of his Father to bear upon all men. Here is the image of the New Man, who enables his brethren to break their self-centered patterns and to make responses which are fitting within the context of God's universal love. Encounters in the past and those anticipated in the future are now reinterpreted in such a way that the present becomes time-full compresence with God and the neighbor in an interaction moving toward eternal life. Men become responsible sons of God. It is in this context of responsible sonship to God that the Christian is to pose his ethical questions, and, as pointed out above, for Niebuhr the context within which an action is taken is more important than the action itself.

Niebuhr discussed the problem of deciding on a particular concrete action in his "Concluding Unscientific Postscript" to *Christ and Culture.* Here he indicated that the decisions of the individual believer are always relative, existential, and made in dependent freedom. They are relative to the amount of his knowledge, the measure of his faith, the historical position he occupies, the duties of his station in society, and his system of values. But his decisions, while relative, are also existential. That is, they cannot be reached by speculative inquiry but must be made in freedom by a responsible subject acting in the present moment on the basis of what is true for him. Nevertheless, although such decisions are individual, they should not be individualistic. Niebuhr was convinced that our decisions ought not be made in lonely internal dialogue but in the living dialogue of the self with other selves, for what is at stake is not our eternal happiness but our responsibility to God for our neighbor. At this point Niebuhr differed sharply with Kierkegaardian existentialism, which he considered to be a prime representative of individualistic thinking, and advocated in its stead what he termed "social existentialism," that is, an understanding of existence which recognizes the social character of the self as well as the historical nature of its present and the historical character of Christ.

Niebuhr's final point concerning the decisions of the individual believer is that the freedom in which they are made is a dependent freedom, dependent on orgins not in our control and on consequences not in our power. "Our ultimate question in this existential situation of dependent freedom," he declared, "is not whether we will choose in accordance with reason or by faith, but whether we will choose with reasoning faithlessness or reasoning faith" (CC, 251). That is, do we make our choices as men whose existence is finally dependent on undependable chance or as men who, because of Jesus Christ and his faithfulness, have come to trust in God as the source and ground and government and end of all things and to be loyal to him and to his cause of universal creation and universal redemption, and to all others who are loyal to this cause? Niebuhr believed that it is as men of faith that we should make our ethical decisions as responsive, responsible beings. He summed up his position in these words:

> To make our decisions in faith is to make them in view of the fact that no single man or group or historical time is the church; but that there is a church of faith in which we do our partial, relative

work and on which we count. It is to make them in view of the fact that Christ is risen from the dead, and is not only the head of the church but the redeemer of the world. It is to make them in view of the fact that the world of culture—man's achievement—exists within the world of grace—God's Kingdom (CC, 256).

III

Some Critical Questions

My purpose till now has been to disclose the main facets and to reflect something of the wholeness of the thought of H. Richard Niebuhr. I realize, of course, that no attempt at summarization or systematization can succeed in capturing all the richness of his insight and the breadth of his concern, and I am aware that little attention has been paid to questions of change and development in his theology. As a result, a certain amount of eclecticism and harmonization has been unavoidable. Nevertheless, I believe that the presentation has been adequate to allow the reader to form a responsible judgment regarding Niebuhr's basic theological and ethical convictions. I now turn to the question of what elements seem most problematic to critics of Niebuhr's thought, and I do so with the full realization that we are not dealing with a theologian who has dropped into the past but with one who is still very much our contemporary.

One of the most frequent criticisms of Niebuhr's theology concerns his view of history and his thoroughgoing commitment to a historicist perspective in theology and ethics. History has to do with the ordering and meaning of temporal events, and the theologian who commits himself to "doing theology" exclusively within the realm of history must thereafter work in a medium in which there are no absolutes but only relativity and change, no "events-in-themselves" but only events that are related to other events and witnessed to by human subjects. When Niebuhr accepted the confines of the realm of history, did he not relinquish any possibility of being a *theo*-logian, since theologians by ordinary definition must deal with the God who transcends history? Further, did he by accepting historical relativism forfeit any possibility of objectivity in matters of truth and fall inevitably into the morass of subjectivism and irrationalism? From the standpoint of the Christian metaphysician, Niebuhr the historicist seems both unable and unwilling to do justice to the *being* of God or of man. After all, since God *is* and man *is*, must we not speak of their *reality* quite apart from their relationship to us? Is *being* not prior to *meaning*? Should not the theologian make ontological judgments as well as historical ones? Must he not analyze what something (or someone) is in and for itself? Is there not a truth of reason that stands firm against the tides of history?

On the other hand, criticism of Niebuhr's historism (the term he apparently preferred to "historicism") can come not only from the side of metaphysicians but also from that of historians, some of whom believe his distinction between internal and external history is an oversimplification which too easily allows subjective interpretation to outweigh objective facts or events. Is it really possible to divide history into inner and outer aspects depending upon whether one participates in it "existentially" or observes it "disinterestedly?" If Christian revelation is actually historical, then is it recognized and known only by those who "participate" in this history by "faith," or is revelation "there" in history to be seen and known by everyone who has eyes to see? If one asserts that revelation is history, can one also say that history is revelation? And if one assumes, with Niebuhr, that revelation occurs only as one participates through faith in the revelatory history, i.e., the history of Jesus Christ, then how is it possible ever to communicate about revelation with those who do not have faith? Furthermore, when Christians are confronted by non-Christians who also claim to have knowledge of a revelation of God, then what criteria could possibly be adduced to judge between revelations?

Closely connected with Niebuhr's concept of history is the view of faith as trust and fidelity. Just as revelation is historical in the sense that it is related to *me* (inner history), so faith is interpreted in interpersonal terms. While few would dispute the face that faith in the Christian tradition involves personal trust, the question arises as to whether Niebuhr does justice to the intellectual content of faith. Is there no *knowledge* inherent in faith, no beliefs *about* God that are intrinsic to any belief *in* God? Does not Niebuhr's view of faith actually denigrate human reason, that grand capability of man that distinguishes him from the lower animals? Does faith not demand the use of clear concepts, so that faith would rightly involve the acceptance of certain statements as true? Is it possible to reduce the concept of faith to person-to-person or I-Thou relationships without losing the dimension of rational objectivity and thus falling again into irrationality and subjectivism?

From yet another quarter Niebuhr's understanding of faith is questioned by those who believe that Christian faith is *sui generis.* Niebuhr speaks of faith as a general category and even claims that everyone lives by faith. That is, every human being places his trust in something that makes his life worth living. But is this generalized concept of faith what the New Testament means by "faith"? Does not (Christian) faith refer exclusively to an occurrence in the life of man which is produced by an action of God and which is therefore unique and incomparable? Is not the event of faith directly correlated with the revelation of God in Jesus Christ through the work of the Holy Spirit, so that Christian faith stands without analogy to any other concept of faith? Then faith would be an event the objectivity of which is wholly dependent on God, and no naturally constituted polar relationship between God and man is thinkable and no generally recognized understanding of faith is adequate.

Still another objection raised against Niebuhr's view of faith involves the allegation that faith for him is essentially a value-judgment. That is, faith in God is nothing more than man's own judgment about what makes his life worth living. If this is true, if God is defined in terms of human values, then what is to prevent "God" from being a mere projection of man's desires? Then faith would have no transcendent reference, and the question of God's *being*— quite apart from man—would be begged. Here we return to the question of whether God can be thought of only in relation to man. Must not God's being be given priority over his meaning or his value for man? Niebuhr refused to discuss the aseity of God, that is, his being in and for himself, but did he not thereby impoverish his doctrine of God? In his self-revelation does God not reveal his true self? Is he not in himself who he is in his revelation? And in his revelation is he not *other* than man, declaring who he is apart from all human value-judgments? To be sure, unless we choose to describe God in terms of negation (God is *not* finite, *not* mortal, etc.), we must resort to analogical description (God is *like* a father, *like* a king, etc.), but even so, must we not attempt to set forth God's uniqueness, his being unlike man, his radical freedom from man as well as for man?

The uniqueness of God, according to the mainline tradition of the church, is manifest in his triunity, that is, in his being one God in three distinguishable but inseparable "persons" or "modes of being": Father, Son, and Holy Spirit. In the light of this tradition, the question can be asked of Niebuhr whether, with his tremendous emphasis on monotheism, he does justice to the doctrine of God as Trinity. Niebuhr has well depicted the problem of unitarianisms of the first, second, and third "persons" of the Trinity, but has he himself been able to formulate an understanding of God that escapes the charge of unitarianisms? Niebuhr never tired of stressing God's oneness, but is the oneness predicated in abstraction from God's revelation in Christ? In Niebuhr's view, God's oneness seems to be that of "being itself," the One beyond (as well as in and through) the many, whereas the traditional Christian doctrine of God witnesses to a oneness of God which is manifest precisely in God's self-revelation. Or to say it another way: the Christian doctrine of the Trinity was formulated by the church in order to preserve the *unity* of God, who is at one and the same time Father, Son, and Holy Spirit. Niebuhr's concept of God, which postulates a "Trinity" as a result of certain activities of God in the world, appears unable to measure up to the venerable Trinitarian rule that "the activities of the Trinity in relation to the world are *undivided.*"

A further question concerning Niebuhr's understanding of God is whether he has successfully combined the idea of God as "Being Itself" with the notion of God as "First Person." Is it possible to apply to God at one and the same time the most universal and abstract of concepts and the most specific and particular of concepts? Can Being Itself, or the Ground of Being, be personal, or better, a Person? These symbols seem to be incompatible, and yet Niebuhr chose to use them both, despite the tension this involved. One is tempted to ask why he did not use the concept of "Creator" rather than "Being Itself," since "Creator" does not have pantheistic overtones, clearly distinguishes between God and his creation, and is readily combined with the concept of personhood. Also, creatorship implies sovereignty, an attribute which for Niebuhr was the *sine qua non* of deity.

Niebuhr's belief in the sovereignty of God is itself subject to question. First, one might ask whether this belief is more than naïve optimism. In face of the evil experienced by man in the world, how can Niebuhr affirm that the world is good? How dare he speak of confidence in God's almighty and benevolent governance of the world in the light of cancer, earthquake, and man's ever-present inhumanity to man? If God controls history, as Niebuhr affirms, then is God good? Would it not be better simply to recognize the ongoing problem of evil and to speak more in terms of God's suffering rather than his sovereignty? Second, if God controls history, is man free? Is man caught in a historical determinism whereby whatever happens must be interpreted as the will of God? Niebuhr would certainly not wish to affirm this, but is it the logic of his position?

From his standpoint as a confessing Christian, Niebuhr refused to raise the question of the existence of God. That is, as a man of faith he accepted God's existence as axiomatic, and for the most part he also refused to take with seriousness any professions of atheism. In Niebuhr's view every man places his faith in some "ultimate" or "god" which makes his life worth living, which means that man's problem is really not atheism but idolatry. Only late in Niebuhr's career does this conviction begin to waver, when he begins to ask whether modern men have actually become nihilists who no longer even trust their gods. In the light of subsequent developments, such as the "death-of-God" movement, is it not legitimate to criticize Niebuhr for failing to face the problem of atheism more squarely and to deal more adequately with the problems involved in the Christian affirmation that "God is"? In this connection, should he not have elaborated on his more or less unexplained affirmations, first, of a kind of natural knowledge—or at least awareness—of God, and, second, of his trust in God prior to his acknowledgment of the lordship of Christ?

Just as Niebuhr's doctrine of the Trinity can be challenged from a traditional point of view, so can his Christology. In accordance with his historicist perspective, Niebuhr began his thinking about Jesus Christ from "below" rather than from "above," that is, he began with the man Jesus rather than the pre-existent Second Person of the Trinity. Since he considered the notion of Christ's pre-existence as an unwarranted speculative idea, he could not accept the traditional doctrine of incarnation or the orthodox view that in the person of Jesus Christ were united two natures, one divine and one human. There can be no doubt that Niebuhr believed Jesus to be truly man, but one can question whether, or at least in what sense, he believed Jesus to be truly God. Does he believe Jesus to be an adopted Son of God? Does he look upon Jesus as embodying certain virtues, as when he speaks of his incarnating faith? Does Niebuhr believe Jesus' difference from other men is a matter of degree or of kind? Niebuhr points to the resurrection as being a sign of Jesus' uniqueness as Lord, but what does he mean by "resurrection"? Is it an event of inner and outer history, or only of the former, that is, the occurrence of the rise of faith in the disciples? Whether or not Jesus Christ can be called truly God by Niebuhr is a question, but he surely believed that Jesus mediated the divine to man. But did he believe that only the divine can mediate God, or did he believe that the human is able to perform this mediation?

Many additional questions could be posed, but I shall limit myself to only one more, which has to do with Niebuhr's ethics. To what extent does Niebuhr's embrace of historical relativism preclude his recognition and employment of objective norms and principles in ethics? Is he an advocate of "situational ethics" in which the crucial element in the ethical decision is the subject's assessment of the situation, or does he support the use of ethical rules and maxims? Perhaps the entire debate over situational *versus* normative ethics is a "misplaced debate" (James Gustafson), but the question as to whether Niebuhr's position is to be understood as "subjective relativism" or as "objective relatedness" (Paul Ramsey) is still relevant. What is the role of the law in the determination of what is the fitting or responsible action in any given situation? Also, is Niebuhr right in his insistence that for Christian ethics the determination of the context is more important than that of the content of ethical action?

Most of these "critical questions" that have been raised

are not new. A perusal of the various writings about H. Richard Niebuhr, which are listed in the bibliography at the conclusion of this book, will disclose these and many more. Niebuhr was well aware of his critics' questions, and I believe he had some of them in mind when in 1960, two years prior to his death, he wrote "Reformation: Continuing Imperative," his oft-quoted reflections on his theological pilgrimage and apology for his Christian concerns. His special concern, he explained, had always been the reformation of the church, whereas his brother Reinhold, to whom he claimed to be indebted for many things but whom he cites very little in his writings, had devoted himself mainly to the reform of culture, which is one of the church's never-ending responsibilities. Rather than try to answer H. Richard Niebuhr's critics for him, perhaps it is better to give attention to some of his remarks in this essay. Even though he does not answer all the questions directly, he alludes to most of the theological and ethical issues that have been raised and, at the same time, he clearly delineates the positions from which he would be very reluctant to yield ground.

First, we should recall the three convictions which Niebuhr considered to be fundamental for him, namely, that God is sovereign, which meant for him that Being Itself is trustworthy; that man is lost, sinful, and idolatrous; and that trust in God, the Ground of Being, and enlistment in his cause of universal creation and universal redemption are miraculous gifts. The sovereignty of God, the lostness of man, and the gift of forgiveness through faith—these form the hard core of Niebuhr's theology, and we should recognize that they represent basic themes of the Protestant Reformation. These convictions were forged during the early thirties when Niebuhr broke with liberal or empirical theology, and together they form his answer to the question of theodicy. Niebuhr came to believe that man in his lostness cannot define the good and then predicate this of God; instead, man must learn from God who he is and what is good. And what does man learn? In spite of all appearances to the contrary, Being Itself is good, life is good, and God's purpose as it is being worked out in history is good. How can anyone believe this? Niebuhr answered:

How is it possible to rely on God as inconquerably loving and redeeming, to have confidence in him as purposive person working towards the glorification of his creation and of himself in his works, to say to the great "It": "Our Father who art in heaven"—this remains the miraculous gift.[1]

We must now ask what Jesus Christ has to do with these basic convictions about God and man. The answer is that for Niebuhr himself Jesus Christ is utterly inseparable from these convictions, for so far as he could see, the miracle of faith in God has been wrought among men by and through Jesus Christ. Nevertheless, he confessed that he had no evidence that the miracle is worked *only* by Jesus Christ and that it has never been given outside the sphere of his working. Several things appear to be involved in Niebuhr's attitude. First, he apparently had noted what he considered to be the presence of faith in God among persons who were not seemingly affected by Jesus Christ, and in such cases he said that he simply posited "the presence also of something like Jesus Christ." The second factor is Niebuhr's dislike of the tendency among Christians to make of Christ an occasion for pride and self-aggrandizement and to fail to rejoice when evidence of faith in God is found in those who would not call themselves Christians. Is not the crucial thing trust and loyalty to the One beyond the many and fidelity to the cause of reconciliation? When signs of this are detected *extra muros*, why should Christians not rejoice that the grace of God which they know in and through Jesus Christ is a grace that knows no bounds?

A third factor has to do with the priorities involved in the Christian community's own confession of faith. Regarding these, Niebuhr declared: "In my confession of faith, as in that of many men I know, the expression of trust in God and the vow of loyalty to him comes before the acknowledgement of Christ's lordship."[2] Niebuhr seems to be reminding us that, regardless of the fact that the Christian's knowledge of God has come through Jesus Christ, his confession of faith, as, for example, in the Apostles' Creed, is first in God the Father and then in Christ as Lord. The lordship that has been bestowed upon the risen Christ stems from the sovereign God, Maker of heaven and earth.

Another factor involved in Niebuhr's view of Jesus Christ is his historism. He was convinced of the radically historical character of human existence, which meant that he could see and believe only as a self in time. This methodological conviction, which he said had come to him from liberalism or perhaps from modern existence as such, focused his thought on the Jesus who lived in history and whom he had come to know in his own history. He admitted that, living after Jesus Christ, he could realize the possibility of a pre-existent, eternal Christ or a second person of the Trinity, but in his judgment such speculation ends in a theoretical theology that not only assumes an unwarranted vantage point above history but is also nonproductive of true faith. Faith, Niebuhr declared, does not come through doctrines about what lies behind the historical event. "It comes to me in history," he said, "not in doctrines about history."[3] To be consistent, it seems to me that he should have said that it comes in history and not in doctrines, whether about history or about that which lies behind, above, or beyond history.

Involved in this historism is the sharp distinction Niebuhr drew between experience and doctrine, between personal relations and ideas, between the basis of faith and expressions of faith. For him personal relations were more important than anything else. It was not that theological formulations were unimportant, for they have their rightful place in the ongoing effort of faith to understand and express itself. It was, rather, that for Niebuhr faith was the crucial matter, and faith stems from personal encounter between selves and involves primarily interpersonal trust and loyalty, not intellectual assent to teaching or doctrine. For this reason Niebuhr refused to define the Christian life in terms of right believing or Christianity as the true religion. In his opinion, these definitions place the accent in the wrong place. "Right believing" fails to do justice to what is essential in faithful living: the existential, personal experience of encounter and interaction, the I-Thou relations between God and man and between man and man. To speak of Christianity as "the true religion" sounds to him like idolatry and henotheism, "the worship of one god who is however the god of an ingroup rather than the ground of all being."[4]

This brings us to another element in Niebuhr's thought that needs to be highlighted, namely, his belief that human society and culture requires continual reformation and conversion. The sovereignty of God calls for a radically monotheistic faith, but there is in man a sinful tendency toward the deification of lesser gods or of an ingroup god. Niebuhr emphasized that this tendency operates in the churches and in religions as well as in any other part of human culture; all are "subject to a constant process of reformation and deformation, or *metanoia* (repentance) and fall."[5] Admitting that his concern over the years had been more the reform of the church than the reform of culture, Niebuhr pointed out that whereas in his earlier years his protestations were directed against the presence within the church of the alien spirits of capitalism, nationalism, Communism, and technological civilization, in his later years he was forced to protest the church's own idolatrous attachment to itself, to the Bible, and even to Christ. To put this later protest in proper perspective, it is probably wise to quote his own words:

In many circles today we have substituted for the religion-centered faith of the nineteenth century a church-centered faith, as though the historical and visible church were the representative of God on earth, as though the Bible were the only word that God is speaking. I do not see how we can witness to the divine sovereignty without being in the church nor how we can understand what God is doing and declaring to us in our public and private experience without the dictionary of the Scriptures, but it seems to me that in our new orthodox movements we are moving dangerously near to the untenable positions against which the Reformation and the eighteenth century revival had to protest.[6]

It is at the end of his reflections that Niebuhr calls for a resymbolization of the Christian message and the life of faith in the One God. He pictured Western men and women as living in a great religious void, disillusioned with their gods and experiencing a great emptiness, and in this situation he confessed that he was haunted by the phrase: "the hungry sheep look up and are not fed." He believed that the old symbols—"Word of God," "redemption," "incarnation," "justification," "grace," "eternal life"—had become worn out and thus were no longer able either to grasp or to communicate the reality of our existence before God. Resymbolization is impossible, he said, "unless one has direct relations in the immediacy of personal life to the actualities to which people in another time referred with the aid of such symbols."[7]

IV

The Promise of
H. Richard Niebuhr

It is obvious from the critical questions and from Niebuhr's remarks, as these were presented in the previous chapter, that Niebuhr's theology does not fit neatly into any of the familiar theological patterns. We now must ask precisely what theological position Niebuhr does hold. If he fits no established pattern, then one can conclude either that his theology is an anomalous mishmash that defies definition or that he was forging something new in the world of Christian theology. If one assumes the latter to be the case—and I do—then what is the new creation? It seems to me that Niebuhr himself has designated two essential ingredients in his thought: first, his radical monotheism, and, second, his social existentialism. Perhaps, then, his theology could be called a socio-existential monotheism. However, to be fair to Niebuhr we would need to affix the adjective "Christian," because Jesus Christ is by no means incidental to his theology but is decisive for it. Thus we would end with what is admittedly a rather cumbersome and yet descriptive label: Christian socio-existential monotheism.

What are the basic features of this theology? First, its center is the One God, the personal Ground of Being to whom all beings are related and from whom they derive their existence, worth, and purpose. Second, it is a theology of triadic relationship between God, self, and neighbor, where none can be thought of apart from the others. Third, it conceives of man as responsive and responsible; he is the creature called to respond to God in trust and loyalty and to be responsible to God for the world, which includes not only his human neighbors but the entire universe of being. Fourth, its major symbol for providing an understanding of God and man and of the meaning of life is Jesus of Nazareth, who demonstrated in his life, words, deeds, and destiny what it means to be a son of God and to love one's neighbor. Fifth, it recognizes man's proclivity to sin by being unfaithful to God and unloving to his neighbor, and it calls for a continuous repentance and reformation of human life. Sixth, it conceives of the church as those human beings who commit themselves to resymbolize in word and deed the life of Jesus Christ as an ongoing witness and summons to the world. And seventh, it believes that God is the sovereign Lord of history whose kingdom is ruled by mercy and moves ineluctably toward its goal of universal redemption.

If I have rightly named Niebuhr's theology and have accurately depicted its essential elements, then we must admit that it does differ from traditional interpretations of Christianity. It is not the story of a supernatural being, the Second Person of the Trinity, who becomes incarnate by assuming human flesh, performs during his lifetime many miracles, atones for the sins of all mankind by suffering death on a cross, rises bodily from the grave, ascends into heaven where he sits at the right hand of God and from whence he will someday return to judge the living and the dead. I believe it would be unfair to Niebuhr to picture him as unsympathetic to the intention of this particular interpretation of Christianity. Nevertheless, he considered it too speculative and mythological to bear the freight of the Christian message for today. Furthermore, he found in the Bible itself a more satisfactory framework for interpreting the meaning of Christian faith, namely, the prophetic tradition of the Old Testament, with its message of the righteousness of the One God who demands that the People of God be faithful, just, and merciful; and the Synoptic tradition of the New Testament, with its picture of the man Jesus, who proclaims the coming of the kingdom of God and who in his words, deeds, death, and destiny manifests the meaning of the kingdom, revealing the character of God and the true life of man.

Niebuhr was haunted by the vision of the hungry sheep who looked up and are not fed. He was passionately concerned that the church meet the real needs and answer the real questions of men and women in the twentieth century. He believed that the question people were asking was not so much, "How can I find a gracious God?" but "How can I find a meaning-giving God?" or "How can I find a gracious neighbor?" or "What is our hope for attaining peace and justice in our life together on earth?" Although he never worked out a "systematic theology," there is an amazing consistency at the point of his deepest concerns and convictions. Certainly his thought is rich with insight and thus with promise.

There is a sense in which the demonstration of Niebuhr's promise would require the repetition of the exposition of his thought, for relevant insights are to be found in almost everything he wrote. For example, his exposure of the sins of denominationalism in his very first book is as relevant today for the question of church union as it was in 1929. However, rather than attempting to sift the materials and to pick out the numerous promising elements along the way, we shall limit ourselves here to a brief presentation of some of those facets of his thought that seem to be unusually pregnant with promise.

The first is his call for a lack of defensiveness among Christians. The other side of this coin might be called his nonapologetic confessionalism, but I prefer to put it the other way in order to make the point. It is past time for

Christians to cease being defensive about their theological formulations, as if these formulations were the truth of God himself. This does not mean that doctrine and confessional statements are unimportant or that the ongoing task of formulating doctrine is any less necessary for the apostolic function of the church, but it means that our theological formulations are relative to time, place, and culture; that they never adequately represent the living truth of persons and personal relationships; that they are expressions of faith rather than the basis of faith; that claims of exclusiveness and superiority breed intolerance and pride and thus often thwart the hearing of the Christian message; and that in our dialogue with others we must have an open-minded theology and be willing to listen. Niebuhr's nondefensive attitude and spirit in no way lessened his concern for his basic convictions or for the mission of the church, but it made him sensitive to the problem of ideologization, open to truth wherever he found it, and confident that God does not require our defense, but only our witness.

A second promising element I wish to highlight is Niebuhr's understanding of faith, particularly his insistence that faith involves not only trust of another (the passive aspect) but loyalty to the other and to the other's cause (the active aspect). This emphasis on fidelity or loyalty catches up the notion of active discipleship and places it squarely within an interpersonal understanding of faith. Although I think Niebuhr should have given more attention to the problem of the content of faith, I can only rejoice that he made it absolutely clear that the Christian is called in his faith not simply to enjoy God but also to serve him.

One of the most prominent and promising elements in Niebuhr's theology is his uncompromising and radical monotheism, both in its positive and in its negative meaning. Positively, it means that only the One God, who alone is eternal and absolute and infinite, is to be worshiped and served. Negatively, it means the prohibition of the absolutizing of anything or anyone less than God and yet, at the same time, the reverencing of every relative existent. According to Niebuhr, the two great mottoes of radical monotheism are these: "I am the Lord thy God; thou shalt have no other gods before me" and "Whatever is, is good." The corollary, then, of radical monotheism is radical faith and universal loyalty. Seldom has theology been presented a more useful notion than radical monotheism, for it enables us both to unmask our polytheisms and henotheisms, inside and outside the church, and also to detect tendencies toward monotheistic faith in the life of our political, scientific, and other communities.

The radicalism of Niebuhr's conception of monotheism becomes evident when he distinguishes it from humanism (a kind of henotheism in which humanity is a closed society), from naturalism (another closed-society faith which does not recognize that being is greater in extent than nature), and from Albert Schweitzer's principle of "reverence for life" (a henotheism of the community of the living). In Niebuhr's view, the neighbor we are to love is not the one who is near us in our interest group *when* he is near us in that passing association (polytheism) nor our fellows in the closed society (henotheism), but our companions in being. Thus, radically monotheistic faith has implications not only for our treatment of fellow human beings, both near and far, but also for our treatment of animals, plants, and even inorganic matter.

In *Radical Monotheism and Western Culture* Niebuhr gives several illustrations of the meaning of monotheistic faith in different areas of human activity. In dealing with the political issue of religious freedom it means the acknowledgment that loyalty to God is prior to every civic loyalty, that before man is a member of any political society he is a member of the universal commonwealth in which he is under obligations that take precedence over all duties to the state, and that the state must therefore acknowledge men's rights to perform such duties. On the question of the powers of a democratic government, it means that the voice of the people is not the voice of God (henotheistic democracy) and that no relative power (whether nation, people, or tyrant) can claim absolute sovereignty or complete loyalty. In the realm of science, radical faith is exercised when scientists rise above national loyalties and make universal truth their cause.

Niebuhr believed that in our day radical monotheistic faith must often struggle against two forms of henotheism within Christianity itself, namely, a church-centered faith that identifies the church with God and church history with holy history, and, second, a Christ-centered faith that makes Jesus Christ the absolute center of confidence and loyalty, substitutes the lordship of Christ for the lordship of God, and turns theology into Christology. Niebuhr spelled out his objections to the latter in this passage:

> To be a Christian now means not so much that through the mediation and the pioneering faith of Jesus Christ a man has become wholly human, has been called into membership in the society of universal being, and has accepted the fact that amidst the totality of existence he is not exempt from the human lot; it means rather that he has become a member of a special group, with a special god, a special destiny, and a separate existence (RMWC, 60).

What Niebuhr is protesting is the idea that Jesus Christ as the revelation of God means the disclosure of a private God, when in fact it means the disclosure that the valuing, saving power in the world is the principle of Being Itself, that the principle of Being gives, maintains, and re-establishes worth, and that men are called to make the redemptive cause of God their own cause.

Other elements of Niebuhr's theology that hold unusual promise are his Christology, particularly his view of Jesus Christ as the moral son of God who is shown in his virtues to be the mediating and focusing point between two movements: from man to God and from God to man; his concept of man has *homo dialogicus*, an answerer whose very being is constituted by his relationship to God and to other selves; his "ethics of the fitting," which he developed within the context of man's responsibility; his view of Christ as the converter or transformer of culture and of revelation as the permanent revolution of our human religion; his conception of the church as a pioneering community whose purpose is the increase among men of the love of God and neighbor; his understanding of the ordained minister as "pastoral director," with the concomitant emphasis on the fact that the ministry is the responsibility of the entire church; his view of the kingdom of God as the hidden rule in all of life which keeps man open to the future and filled with hope; his emphasis on the covenant relationship between God and man; and his faith in universal redemption, in basic agreement with F. D. Maurice's assertion that "the abyss of love is deeper than the abyss of death."

In conclusion I wish to speak of Niebuhr's catholic vision. In 1948 he published an article with the title, "The Gift of the Catholic Vision," and in it he maintained that in our day theology has been blessed by the receipt of a precious gift, the gift of the catholic vision. He proposed that the gift had come from many historical sources and was essentially an ecumenical vision with universal horizons. It involves a view of that which is objective and over against us, namely, the revelation of God in Christ and his kingdom. It is a vision that encompasses the work and contributions of the entire catholic community throughout the history of the church, inclusive not only of time and space but of special functions and special views; and while it is a vision given to the church, it is at the same time a vision that extends beyond the church to the sovereignty of God over the entire world. It was Niebuhr's hope that this catholic vision would being a new wholeness and catholicity into theological education and would lead to new approaches to perennial theological questions. He hoped it would eventuate in a doctrine of God that would overcome our unitarianisms, in a doctrine of the atonement that is based on the objectivity of an event and a process that concerns not only the community of the church but also the community of mankind, and in a doctrine of the church that would see the human response to divine action as something more inclusive and more strange than a religious association. When Niebuhr contemplated the mystery and the wonder of the church from this perspective, he wrote these words:

> Its members forever transcend the boundaries of what men call religion; they form sects, societies within society yet apart from society; they enter restlessly into the political and economic life of the civilizations in which they dwell; they seek a Zion which cannot be located in any part of earth and yet are not content to find their beatitude one by one in a heavenly Paradise. It is a pilgrim community which makes strangely enduring settlements. It is an abnormal community which does not fit into this world and yet forever seeks to make itself at home in a world that is a Fatherland. It has a King and a law of its own, to which it appeals beyond all the rulers and laws of men, but the King is invisible and the law is impractical; and yet, all other kinds are powerless before him and all the laws save his impractical.[1]

It seems to me that H. Richard Niebuhr, in all his endeavors in the fields of Christian theology and ethics, displayed to a remarkable degree that gift of the catholic vision of which he spoke and that he belonged indubitably to that church which he so eloquently envisioned.

Key to Abbreviations

CC: *Christ and Culture*
KGA: *The Kingdom of God in America*
MR: *The Meaning of Revelation*
PCM: *The Purpose of the Church and Its Ministry*
RMWC: *Radical Monotheism and Western Culture*
RS: *The Responsible Self*
SSD: *The Social Sources of Denominationalism*

Notes

Chapter II. Niebuhr's Thought

1. Whitehead, *Religion in the Making* (New York: The Macmillan Co., 1926), pp. 16f.
2. Tillich, "Existential Thinking in American Theology," in *Religion in Life*, X, No. 3 (Summer 1941), 455.
3. Niebuhr, "A Communication," in *The Christian Century*, XLIX, No. 14 (April 6, 1932), 447.
4. Niebuhr, "The Triad of Faith," in *Andover Newton Bulletin*, XLVII, No. 1 (October 1954), 10.
5. Niebuhr, "Reformation: Continuing Imperative," in *The Christian Century*, LXXVII, No. 9 (March 2, 1960), 249.
6. Niebuhr, "An Attempt at a Theological Analysis of Missionary Motivation," in N.Y.C. Missionary Research Library Occasional Bulletin, XIV, No. 1 (January 1963), pp. 1f.
7. Niebuhr, "Reformation: Continuing Imperative," *op. cit.*, p. 250.
8. *Ibid.*, p. 248.
9. *Ibid.*, p. 249.
10. Niebuhr, "An Attempt at a Theological Analysis of Missionary Motivation," *op. cit.*, p. 3.
11. Niebuhr, "The Norm of the Church," in *Journal of Religious Thought*, IV, No. 1 (Autumn-Winter 1946-1947), 14.
12. Niebuhr, "The Hidden Church and the Churches in Sight," in *Religion in Life*, XV, No. 1 (Winter 1945-1946), 116.
13. *Ibid.*, 112f.
14. Niebuhr, "The Responsibility of the Church for Society," in *The Gospel, the Church and the World*, ed. K. S. Latourette (New York: Harper & Brothers, 1946), p. 129.
15. *Ibid.*, p. 130.
16. Niebuhr, "Theology—Not Queen but Servant," in *Journal of Theology*, XXXV, No. 1 (January 1955), 5.

17. Niebuhr, "Evangelical and Protestant Ethics," in *The Heritage of the Reformation*, ed. E. J. F. Arndt (New York: Richard R. Smith, 1950), p. 20.

18. *Ibid.*, p. 227.

19. *Ibid.*, p. 228.

Chapter III. Some Critical Questions

1. Niebuhr, "Reformation Continuing Imperative," in *The Christian Century*, Vol. LXXVII (March 2, 1960), 249.

2. *Ibid.*, p. 250.

3. *Ibid.*, p. 249.

4. *Ibid.*, p. 250.

5. *Ibid.*

6. *Ibid.*

7. *Ibid.*, p. 251.

Chapter IV. The Promise of H. Richard Niebuhr

1. Niebuhr, "The Gift of the Catholic Vision," in *Theology Today*, IV, No. 4 (January 1948), 520.

A Selected Bibliography

Writings by H. Richard Niebuhr

The Social Sources of Denominationalism. New York: Henry Holt and Company, 1929. (Reprinted, with new preface, Hamden, Conn.: The Shoe String Press, 1954; New York: Meridian Books, 1957.)

"Religious Realism in the Twentieth Century," in *Religious Realism*, ed. D. C. Macintosh. New York: The Macmillan Company, 1931, pp. 413-428.

"The Grace of Doing Nothing," in *The Christian Century*, XLIX (March 23, 1932), 378-380. (See critique by Reinhold Niebuhr: "Must We Do Nothing?" *ibid.* ([March 30, 1932] 415-417. See also answer by H. R. Niebuhr: "A Communication: The Only Way into the Kingdom of God," *ibid.*, [April 6, 1932] 447.)

The Church Against the World, by H. R. Niebuhr, Wilhelm Pauck, and F. P. Miller. Chicago, New York: Willett, Clark & Company, 1935. "The Question of the Church," pp. 1-13; "Toward the Independence of the Church," pp. 123-156.

"Man the Sinner," in *Journal of Religion*, XV (July 1935), 272-280.

The Kingdom of God in America. Chicago, New York: Willett, Clark & Company, 1937. (Reprinted, with new preface, Hamden, Conn.: The Shoe String Press, 1956; New York: Harper Torchbooks, TB49, 1959.)

"Value Theory and Theology," in *The Nature of Religious Experience: Essays in Honor of Douglas Clyde Macintosh*, ed. J. S. Bixler, R. L. Calhoun, and H. R. Niebuhr. New York: Harper & Brothers, 1937, pp. 93-116.

"Life Is Worth Living," in *Intercollegian and Far Horizons*, LVII (October 1939), 3-4, 22.

"The Christian Evangel and Social Culture," in *Religion in Life*, VIII (Winter 1939), 44-49.

The Meaning of Revelation. New York: The Macmillan Company, 1941. (Reprinted, New York: Macmillan Paperbacks Edition, 1960.)

"The Christian Church in the World's Crisis," in *Christianity and Society*, VI (Summer 1941), 11-17.

"The Nature and Existence of God: A Protestant's View," in *motive*, IV (December 1943), 13-15, 43-46.

"The Hidden Church and the Churches in Sight," in *Religion in Life*, XV (Winter 1945-1946), 106-117.

"The Responsibility of the Church for Society," in *The Gospel, the Church and the World*, ed. K. S. Latourette. New York: Harper & Brothers, 1946, pp. 111-133.

"The Doctrine of the Trinity and the Unity of the Church," in *Theology Today*, III (October 1946), 371-384.

"The Norm of the Church," in *Journal of Religious Thought*, IV (Autumn-Winter 1946-1947), 5-15.

"The Gift of the Catholic Vision," in *Theology Today*, IV (January 1948), 507-521.

"The Disorder of Man in the Church of God," in *Man's Disorder and God's Design*, Vol. I: *The Universal Church in God's Design*. New York: Harper & Brothers, 1949, pp. 78-88.

"Evangelical and Protestant Ethics," in *The Heritage of the Reformation: Essays Commemorating the Centennial of Eden Theological Seminary*, ed. E. J. F. Arndt. New York: Richard R. Smith, 1950, pp. 211-229.

Christ and Culture. New York: Harper & Brothers. 1951. (Reprinted, New York: Harper Torchbooks, TB3, 1956.)

"The Center of Value," in *Moral Principles of Action: Man's Ethical Imperative*, ed. R. N. Anshen. New York: Harper & Brothers, 1952, pp. 162-175.

"The Idea of Covenant and American Democracy," in *Church History*, XXIII (June 1954), 126-135.

"Issues between Catholics and Protestants," in *Religion in Life*, XXIII (Spring 1954), 199-205.

"The Triad of Faith," in *Andover Newton Bulletin*, XLVII (October 1954), 3-12.

Christian Ethics: Sources of the Living Tradition. Edited with introductions by Waldo Beach and H. Richard Niebuhr. New York: Ronald Press Company, 1955. Chapters 1, 8, 9, and 13 by Niebuhr.

Theology—Not Queen but Servant," in *Journal of Religion*, XXXV (January 1955), 1-5.

The Purpose of the Church and Its Ministry. Reflections on the Aims of Theological Education, in collaboration with Daniel Day Williams and James M. Gustafson. New York: Harper & Brothers, 1956.

"Sören Kierkegaard," in *Christianity and the Existentialists*, ed. Carl Michalson. New York: Charles Scribner's Sons, 1956, pp. 23-42.

The Advancement of Theological Education, by H. Richard Niebuhr, Daniel Day Williams, and James M. Gustafson. New York: Harper & Brothers, 1957.

Radical Monotheism and Western Culture, with supplementary essays. New York: Harper & Brothers, 1960.

"Reformation: Continuing Imperative," in *The Christian Century*, LXXVII (March 2, 1960), 248-251. (In the series "How My Mind Has Changed.")

"On the Nature of Faith," in *Religious Experience and Truth: A Symposium*, ed. Sidney Hook. New York: New York University Press, 1961, pp. 93-102.

"The Protestant Movement and Democracy in the United States," in *Religion in American Life*, Vol. I: *The Shaping of American Religion*, ed. James Ward Smith and A. Leland Jamison. Princeton, N. J.: Princeton University Press, 1961, pp. 20-71.

The Responsible Self: An Essay in Christian Moral Philosophy, with an Introduction by James M. Gustafson. New York: Harper & Row, 1963.

"An Attempt at a Theological Analysis of Missionary Motivation," in New York City Missionary Research Library Occasional Bulletin, XIV, No. 1 (January, 1963), 1-6. (This article was presented in April, 1951.)

Writings about H. Richard Niebuhr

Ahlstrom, Sidney E. "H. Richard Niebuhr's Place in American Thought," in *Christianity and Crisis*, XXIII (November 25, 1963), 213-217.

Allen, Joseph L. "A Decisive Influence on Protestant Ethics," in *Christianity and Crisis*, XXIII (November 25, 1963), 217-219.

Beker, E. J. "The Sovereignty of God in the Thought of H. Richard

Niebuhr," in *Nederlands Theologisch Tijdschrift*, Vijftiende Jaargang (1960-1961), pp. 108-130.

Buri, Fritz, "The Reality of Faith in H. Richard Niebuhr's *The Meaning of Revelation*," in *How Can We Still Speak Responsibly of God?* Philadelphia: Fortress Press, 1968, pp. 67-83.

Cauthen, Kenneth, "An Introduction to the Theology of H. Richard Niebuhr," in *Canadian Journal of Theology*, X, No. 1 (1964), 4-14.

Cobb, John B., Jr. *Living Options in Protestant Theology*. Philadelphia: The Westminister Press, 1962, pp. 284-301.

Hamilton, Kenneth M. "Trinitarianism Disregarded," in *Encounter*, XXIII (Summer 1962), 343-352.

Harvey, Van A. *The Historian and the Believer*. New York: The Macmillan Company, 1966, pp. 234-342.

Holbrook, Clyde A. "H. Richard Niebuhr," in *A Handbook of Christian Theologians*, ed. Martin E. Marty and Dean G. Peerman. Cleveland and New York: The World Publishing Company, 1965, pp. 375-395.

Macintosh, Douglas Clyde, "Theology, Valuational or Existential?" in *Review of Religion*, IV (November 1939), 23-44.

Phibbs, Raymond C. "An Introductory Summary of the Basic Elements in the Thought of H. Richard Niebuhr," in *Brethren Life and Thought*, V (Autumn 1960), 38-55.

Ramsey, Paul (ed.), *Faith and Ethics: The Theology of H. Richard Niebuhr*. New York: Harper & Brothers, 1957. (Articles by Waldo Beach, Hans W. Frei, James Gustafson, Julian Hartt, Robert S. Michaelsen, Carl Michalson, Liston Pope, Paul Ramsey, and George Schrader.)

Ramsey, Paul, *Nine Modern Moralists*. Englewood Cliffs, N. J.: Prentice-Hall, Inc., 1962, pp. 149-179.

Soper, David Wesley, *Major Voices in American Theology*. Philadelphia: The Westminster Press, 1953, pp. 153-190.

Thelen, Mary Frances, *Man as Sinner in Contemporary American Realistic Theology*. New York: King's Crown Press, 1946, pp. 148-163.

Tillich, Paul, "Existential Thinking in American Theology," in *Religion in Life*, X (Summer 1941), 452-455.

Welch, Claude, "Theology," in *Religion*, ed. Paul Ramsey. Englewood Cliffs, N. J.: Prentice-Hall, Inc., 1965, pp. 262-272.

Williams, Daniel Day, "H. Richard Niebuhr (1894-1962): A Personal and Theological Memoir," in *Christianity and Crisis*, XXIII (November 25, 1963), 209-213.